TRUE CRIME: MISSOURI

TRUE CRIME : MISSOURI

The State's Most Notorious Criminal Cases

David J. Krajicek

STACKPOLE
BOOKS

Published by
STACKPOLE BOOKS
5067 Ritter Road
Mechanicsburg, PA 17055
www.stackpolebooks.com

Printed in the United States of America

10 9 8 7 6 5 4 3 2

FIRST EDITION

Cover design by Tessa J. Sweigert
Cover photos: Hunting dagger, ©Hydromet/Shutterstock. Clockwise, from top left: Ricky Davis, Missouri Department of Corrections photo; Billy "Cock-eyed" Cook, Federal Bureau of Investigation photo; Carl Hall, Missouri Department of Corrections photo; Dena Riley, Missouri Department of Corrections photo; Sni-A-Bar Creek, Lafayette County, Missouri, David J. Krajicek photo; Bonnie Heady, Missouri Department of Corrections photo.

Library of Congress Cataloging-in-Publication Data

Krajicek, David J.
  True crime, Missouri : the state's most notorious criminal cases / David J. Krajicek. — 1st ed.
      p. cm.
  Includes bibliographical references.
  ISBN-13: 978-0-8117-0708-4 (pbk.)
  ISBN-10: 0-8117-0708-3 (pbk.)
  1. Crime—Missouri—Case studies. 2. Criminals—Missouri—Case studies.
I. Title.
  HV6793.M8K73 2011
  364.109778—dc22

                          2011014142

Contents

Introduction

Some years back, a friend of mine found herself living in rural Missouri, after a lifetime spent in the adjacent states of Nebraska and Iowa. As she got to know her new neighbors, my friend began to recognize something distinctly different about people in the Show Me State: They have a scrappy streak of self-reliance when it comes to interpersonal conflict. She witnessed an argument that ended with one man declaring to another, "I have a thousand acres out back, and no one would ever find you!" Another Missourian offered her a piece of advice that she came to regard as a kind of state slogan: "Shoot, shovel, and shut up."

It's not necessarily the sort of motto that the Missouri Division of Tourism might want to adopt. But the fact is that Missourians have always been rather proud of how they stand out from the rest of America. The official state manual describes the native character as "stalwart, conservative, noncredulous." This skeptical, sovereign spirit was famously espoused a century ago by Willard Van Diver, a congressman from the Cape Girardeau area. While giving a speech back East, Van Diver explained, "I come from a state that raises corn and cotton and cockleburs and Democrats, and frothy eloquence neither convinces nor satisfies me. I am from Missouri. You have got to show me."

The state's reputation for being contrary and willing to fight about it goes way back, to long before the quotable Van Diver. Anyone conversant in Missouri crime history will mention William Quantrill, whose pro-Confederate band of guerrilla raiders made the state a forbidding place for Union soldiers. The gang gained infamy during the Civil War for ruthless synchronized attacks on both their opponents and the civilians who supported that side. Quantrill's Raiders served as a trade school for a number of Missourians who went on to storied careers as western outlaws, including Jesse and Frank James, sons of a Baptist minister, and Cole Younger—all three of them born and raised near Kansas City. (Each ended his life in Missouri, as well. Younger and Frank James managed to survive into their dotage. Jesse James did not. He was shot and killed at age thirty-four by his acolyte Robert Ford in a little frame house atop one of the highest hills in St. Joseph, Missouri.)

Missouri bred more than its share of gunslingers and stickup-men in subsequent generations, including the golden age of gangsters, the 1930s. Ma Barker came from Springfield, and the limestone walls outside the doors of majestic Union Station in Kansas City still bear bullet pockmarks from one of the most infamous American gangland shootouts. On June 17, 1933, a group of mugs tried to spring (or silence) bank robber Frank Nash as he was being led by law enforcers out of the train station to a waiting car. An FBI agent, three police officers, and Nash were killed in the "Kansas City Massacre."

* * *

I asked Michael Steiner, a history professor at Northwest Missouri State University, whether it is possible that modern Missouri criminals have some primal link to William Quantrill, Jesse James, Ma Barker, and similar characters.

"The notion that Civil War–era border violence somehow stamped the region with a violent culture strikes me as improbable," he replied. "By the time the war was in full swing, the level of conflict in this region was far less substantial than much of the rest of the country. The infamy of Jesse James tempts this explanation since he ran with border ruffians and became a famed 'outlaw.'"

Yet Steiner and other historians point to an antebellum genesis to help explain the essential Missouri character. Northwest Missouri, in particular, developed a reputation for an ornery populace, and Steiner noted that vast numbers of settlers from Kentucky and Tennessee streamed into that region after the Platte Purchase of 1836. The federal government bought 3,000 square miles of land from Indian tribes, creating the state's nose along the Missouri River in the northwest corner. To this day, there are small pockets there where the local accent sounds more like Memphis than St. Joseph.

"My take is Missouri had a longstanding tradition of violence long before the Civil War era," said Jeffrey Pasley, a University of Missouri–Columbia history professor. "Duels, brawls, and mobs were especially common, back to the first arrival of settlers from the United States in the late eighteenth century. Significant numbers of French, Indians, and the Mormons were dispossessed and driven out by violence. Early settlers were bringing the traditions of slavery and the southern frontier along with them from Kentucky and Tennessee, but it seems to have been particularly raw here. It may have had something to do with the fact that almost all the significant settlements were river towns and essentially border towns, with a highly transient population that was often using St. Louis or Independence or Kansas City as a jumping-off point to hit the trail for someplace farther west."

Pasley said these settlers "were a fairly hard-edged group, involved in rough, exploitative industries like the fur trade, the Indian trade, transportation, outfitting, ranching, and mining." He described them as "the worst of the South and West, rather than what we traditionally think of as the Midwest."

Missouri has always been a gateway state, a crossroads for travelers and itinerants from elsewhere. To begin with, it is one of only two U.S. states that is bordered by eight others. It serves as a nexus point where north, south, east, and west come together. Much of the bottom third of the state, including the Ozarks, has a decidedly southern feel. The northern tier is very much akin to the upper Midwest. And the state's big-city bookends, St. Louis to the east (with a metropolitan population of nearly three million) and Kansas City to the west (metro population of two million), are their own microregions. St. Louis is often called America's westernmost eastern city, and Kansas City the country's easternmost western city. Each has its own rich crime tradition.

"St. Louis in the 1820s, '30s, '40s seems to have been an exceptionally bloody place, from the top to the bottom of the society," Pasley told me. "And in the twentieth century, there was no American city more thoroughly dominated by organized crime than Kansas City."

To this day, he said, Missouri is the most "vice-friendly" of Midwestern states. Simple vices like alcohol and tobacco are lightly taxed and widely available, and the more subterranean vices of narcotics, prostitution, pornography, and gambling are within easy reach. New York's Times Square, Pasley noted, is now more wholesome than the Interstate 70 corridor east of Kansas City.

I asked another friend, a Kansas City writer who has lived in several other Midwestern states, whether there is something unique about criminals in the Show Me State.

"Missouri criminals tend to be sleazier than, say, your average scumbag from Nebraska, Kansas, and Iowa," he said. "I don't have a reference point on the coasts, since I don't follow crime there that closely. I just know there's a real hillbilly, Hell's Angel, slime-bucket vein of humanity that calls the Show Me State home."

Several stories in this collection of infamous Missouri murder cases concern crimes committed by this "vein of humanity," as my colorful friend put it. Raymond and Faye Copeland, geriatric farmers near Chillicothe, quite literally buried the bodies out back. They killed a series of down-and-outers who were drawn into the couple's wacky forgery scheme. And the modern prototype of American vigilantism happened in the northwest Missouri farm hamlet of Skidmore, where citizens shot and killed the town bully, Ken McElroy, and then clammed up about it.

Skidmore, home to just three hundred or so people, has been the site of an unlikely string of sensational crimes, beginning with McElroy's murder. In 2001, twenty-year-old Branson Perry vanished from the town and was never seen again, with foul play suspected. In 2004, a pregnant Skidmore woman named Bobbie Jo Stinnett, twenty-three, was strangled in her home by an acquaintance, Lisa Montgomery. The killer then cut the fetus from Stinnett's womb because she wanted a child herself. The baby survived, miraculously, and Montgomery ended up on death row.

Steiner, the historian from Northwest Missouri State, fifteen miles from Skidmore in Maryville, told me that people in the region have developed "the sense that there is some vortex of evil in Skidmore."

Perhaps it reaches beyond the small town. I asked Thomas Carroll, a keen observer of crime, whether he had seen a pattern of Skidmore's defiant vigilantism more broadly across Missouri, where he had a long career as a professor of criminology and sociology at the University of Missouri–Kansas City. He said he had.

"It does happen in small towns here," Carroll said. "Individual and family honor is highly regarded, and it is protected from within. If someone has dishonored you or your family name, you take care of it yourself. Small towns in Missouri can be very protective of their privacy. It's almost like what you see in the black community. No matter what happens, you don't go to the cops. You don't snitch."

In other words: You shoot, you shovel, and you shut up.

CHAPTER 1
When Stagger Lee Shot Billy

It was after sundown on Christmas Day 1895, and Lee Shelton was prowling the St. Louis tenderloin, puttin' on the dog.

At age thirty-one, Shelton was a well-recognized gadabout in the Deep Morgan, the downtown vice district where he lived, worked, and played. People knew him by the name Stack Lee, probably after a swanky riverboat with that name that passed through St. Louis while plying the Mississippi River to New Orleans.

Always a natty dresser, Stack Lee Shelton had outdone himself for Christmas. His pointy-toed shoes were tricked out with spats and tiny mirrors that shot off shards of reflected lamplight with each stride. He wore a canary-colored shirt, crimson vest, striped gray slacks, and a black overcoat. He gripped a gleaming black cane, and his gigantic cigar left a cloud of blue smoke in his wake. The ensemble was topped by a fine Stetson hat, the classic "Boss of the Plains" style, made of off-white felt.

Shelton turned heads as he strutted along Morgan Street, past taverns, pool halls, burlesque dives, and bawdy houses. At 13th Street, he pushed through the door to Bill Curtis's Saloon. Hollering above the ragtime band and racket, Shelton called out, "Who's buying?" Some jokester pointed him toward Billy Lyons, and Shelton gave his old friend a hearty holiday greeting before they tucked into conversation over strong libations. They had plenty to talk about.

Lyons's brother-in-law was Henry Bridgewater, a saloonkeeper who was one of the wealthiest and most influential black men in St. Louis. Stack Lee Shelton was a businessman, too, of a fashion. Officially, he was a carriage driver and waiter. But everyone knew that he made a living as a pimp—a high-class pimp, but a pimp nonetheless.

Shelton, thirty, was born in Texas in March 1865, during the last weeks of the War Between the States. He was not a big man, at 5-foot-7. But he was lean and mean, and his face, hands, and noggin were carved up like a totem, scars from a lifetime of slashing and slicing—a consequence of his rough trade. He was not easy to stare down, thanks to a crossed left eye that gave him a disquieting glare.

Shelton was in a class of St. Louis sex purveyors known locally as "macks"—a cut above street-corner panderers. He was boss of a fancy whorehouse called the Modern Horseshoe Club.

St. Louis was a big, brawny city in those days—the fourth-largest in America, with a teeming Mississippi River port and ethnic neighborhoods swollen with immigrants and natives alike, especially Germans, Irishmen, Italians, and blacks. They mixed in several ribald districts downtown—the Deep Morgan, Chestnut Valley, and Tamale Town. They were places where any and all citizens could scratch their itch for vices, whether gambling, narcotics, or sex.

The Curtis Saloon was a bull's eye for vice. Newspapers crowed that it "throbbed" with depravity and was the "envy of competitors and terror of the police." One paper said its patrons were "the lower-class of river men and other darkies of the same social status." Stack

Lee Shelton would have harrumphed at the characterization. He thought of himself as an urban dude.

On Christmas night in 1895, two bartenders, Thomas Scott and Frank Boyd, served a crowd of some twenty-five men. The barkeeps would later say that Shelton and Lyons, as longtime friends, had conversed many times and had never been anything but cordial to one another. Yet the men had a history.

Lyons, thirty, was known around the red-light district as a big, burly bully. A native Missourian, he had three young children— Florence, Marie, and Buddy—but was unmarried. He lived with a nephew at 1329 Gay Street, in the midst of the tenderloin. Like most of its denizens, he claimed a legitimate day job as a laborer on the docks at St. Louis's busy waterfront. But Lyons had status in the Deep Morgan through his family connection to saloonkeeper Henry Bridgewater.

Bridgewater was both a ward heeler and fixer for blacks who lived in the district, known as the Bloody Third. His influence was made apparent in 1892, when a man named Charley Brown escaped punishment after murdering another patron, Harry Wilson, inside Bridgewater's Saloon. Brown, Billy Lyons's stepbrother, was a by-marriage shirttail relative of Henry Bridgewater. Wilson, the victim, was a pal of Stack Lee Shelton. That old homicide might have been a festering sore between Lyons and Shelton. And even if it wasn't, there was always politics to argue over.

As in many big cities during that era, black voters were being aggressively courted by both Republicans and Democrats. William Lyons and his brother-in-law, Bridgewater, were Republicans. Bridgewater was the boss of a Republican Club headquartered at his saloon. Stack Lee Shelton was a Democrat, and he lorded over his own club, known as the Colored 400. Its headquarters was just around the corner from Bridgewater's place.

Something caused the holiday chitchat between Shelton and Billy Lyons to take a wrong turn that night. Perhaps it was the old shooting. Perhaps it was politics. Perhaps it was a woman.

It all began with horseplay. The bartenders and several other witnesses would later say that the men pawed at one another's fancy hats. Shelton was wearing his Stetson, while Lyons's topper was a crisp black bowler with a distinctive dome. At some point, Shelton gave Lyons's derby a tomahawk chop with his hand, cleaving the dome and breaking its perfect shape.

"I thought he (Shelton) was playing," said George McFaro, another saloon patron, "and he hauled off and broke his hat, his derby."

The horseplay took an ominous turn over the broken derby. Lyons was furious, and he demanded "six bits"—seventy-five cents—to replace the hat. Lyons swiped the prized Stetson from Shelton's head as collateral. He might as well as have snatched Stack Lee's baby. He loved that damned Stetson.

John Stetson had begun making hats in Philadelphia in 1865. Born in New Jersey, he had grown frustrated by his inability to find a lightweight, durable, rain-resistant hat while traipsing around the mountain West during the 1850s gold rush. In 1865 he began manufacturing his "Boss of the Plains," the prototype cowboy hat made of beaver-fur felt with a crown and brims each measuring four inches. Although they were expensive, that model of Stetson became the gold standard of American hats—and the prized possessions of thousands of western men, from those on the range astride a cayuse to city dudes like Stack Lee Shelton.

Shelton wanted his hat back.

He reached inside his big coat and drew a Smith & Wesson .44. Lyons responded by brandishing an oversized buck knife. The barroom went quiet, and all but a handful of the twenty-five patrons headed for the door. Eyewitness McFaro later recounted the armed exchange between the men.

"If you don't give me my hat," Shelton said, "I will blow your brains out."

"I am not going to give you the hat," Lyons replied. "You cock-eyed son of a bitch, I'm going to make you kill me."

Shelton stepped back a pace or two and squeezed the trigger on the Smith & Wesson, touching off a deafening boom. The slug caught Lyons in the abdomen. He staggered for several seconds, then fell to the barroom floor, mortally wounded but still clutching the Stetson. Shelton leaned over his former friend, yanked the Stetson from his death grip and said, "I told you to give me my hat!" He strutted out the door, walked to his rooming house and checked his weapon with the landlady—following house rules. He then went to bed.

Lyons lingered for about six hours before dying at about 4 A.M. on December 26. Cops named Flanigan and Falvey roused Stack Lee Shelton and arrested him for murder. The landlady turned over the murder weapon. The next day, a brief account of the shooting—with a few errors in spelling and facts—was published in the *St. Louis Globe-Democrat*:

William Lyons, 25, a levee hand, was shot in the abdomen yester-day evening at 10 o'clock in the saloon of Bill Curtis, at Eleventh and Morgan Streets, by Lee Sheldon, a carriage driver.

Lyons and Sheldon were friends and were talking together. Both parties, it seems, had been drinking and were feeling in exu-berant spirits. The discussion drifted to politics, and an argument was started, the conclusion of which was that Lyons snatched Shel-don's hat from his head.

The latter indignantly demanded its return. Lyons refused, and Sheldon withdrew his revolver and shot Lyons in the abdomen. When his victim fell to the floor Sheldon took his hat from the hand of the wounded man and coolly walked away.

He was subsequently arrested and locked up at the Chestnut Street Station. Lyons was taken to the Dispensary, where his wounds were pronounced serious. Lee Sheldon is also known as "Stag" Lee.

The paper later ruefully noted that the shooting of Lyons was one of five in St. Louis that Christmas Day. And it was one of countless barroom shootings in American history, before and since—one drink too many, an insult, a moment of intemperance, a weapon at hand, and a lump of regret lying dead on the floor. Yet the simple story of that barroom shooting managed to enter our national lore as the night that Stack Lee—which became Stack-O Lee, then Stagger Lee—shot Billy Lyons.

It probably began in St. Louis as a realistic story, a narrative ballad that grew through embellishment—akin to tales of northern woodsman Paul Bunyan, train engineer Casey Jones, Tennessee's Davy Crockett, western gunslinger Billy the Kid, frontier fruit Johnny Appleseed, or John Henry, the "steel-drivin' man" who competed against a steam shovel.

The story of Stack Lee moved down the Mississippi River and up its tributaries, like an oral diaspora. By 1897, a black piano man appearing in Kansas City was promoted as planning to play "Stack-a-Lee in variations."

The tune was heard in Colorado in 1899, and a version called the "Ballad of Stackerlee" surfaced in Memphis in 1903. In 1910, a Texas woman sent John Lomax, the itinerant American musicologist, an eight-stanza version of "The Ballad of Stagalee." She added a footnote: "This song is sung by the Negroes on the levee while they are loading and unloading the river freighters."

Music historians have tracked down versions that include as many as forty stanzas, taking the story from Stagger Lee's birth to his death, with a number of ribald stops along the way. Yet through the scores of variations and hundreds of rhyming couplets, one detail is found in virtually every version of the narrative: Shelton's beloved Stetson hat.

"What does the Stagolee epic really say?" singer-songwriter Bob Dylan once asked. "It says a man's hat is his crown."

Author Cecil Brown said the hat was a stand-in for personal dignity. He said the simple shooting became an American fable because Lee Shelton was willing to defend himself. He wrote that Shelton felt "his dignity was at stake," and by striking out he became an archetype for the tough black man who should not be taken lightly.

In 1923, Fred Waring's Pennsylvanians, a popular college jazz band, made a recording of the "Stack O'Lee Blues" that became a hit record. Two years later, Ma Rainey recorded it—and the tune never faded. The melody gradually transformed itself from a slow ballad with complex, jazzy chord changes to the familiar three-chord, I-IV-V blues progression.

To date, more than four hundred artists have recorded a version of Stagger Lee, including, most prominently, Lloyd Price's 1959 recording of "Stagger Lee" that was a number-one U.S. hit and an early crossover from race music to rock and roll—sixty-four years after the shooting.

And what became of Stack Lee Shelton?

The Curtis Saloon bartenders and several customers who witnessed the shooting were called to court for an inquest on December 27, 1895, two days after the shooting. When he arrived, Stack Lee Shelton was greeted by three hundred angry Republican hecklers—members of Henry Bridgewater's political club.

The barroom eyewitnesses recounted what they saw—saloon joshing that seemed to turn deadly over nothing more than hat injury—and Shelton found himself charged with first-degree murder. He posted $4,000 bail and hired Nat Dryden, one of Missouri's most renowned defense attorneys, an indication of his financial well-being.

Meanwhile, a St. Louis newspaper published a story citing information from an informant that the barroom shooting was motivated by revenge for the homicide three years earlier that involved Lyons's kin and Shelton's friend. The story touched off an exchange of letters to the editor from the competing political clubs.

An officer of Shelton's alliance wrote, "The Four Hundred was organized for the moral and physical culture of young colored men. We contemplate no acts of violence, and as law-biding citizens and voters we stand ready and willing to protect the laws of our city, State and the United States. Mr. Lee was our captain. We deeply regret the situation into which our unfortunate member and brother has fallen, and he has our heartfelt sympathies, both individually and collectively, and our hope for him is the best."

Shelton claimed self-defense at his murder trial in July 1896. Defense attorney Dryden, known for a theatrical courtroom style that often swayed naïve jurors, managed to nearly outflank the prosecutor, Orrick Bishop. But after twenty-two hours of deliberation, the jury announced a deadlock—seven in favor of second-degree murder, three for acquittal, and two for manslaughter.

Unfortunately for Shelton, Nat Dryden was known to sample the vices of the Deep Morgan, and he died of a drug and alcohol overdose a few weeks before Shelton's retrial. Stack Lee Shelton was convicted of second-degree murder in a second trial late that same summer and was sent away to prison for twenty-five years. He served just half of the sentence, thanks to pressure from St. Louis Democratic bosses. He was paroled on Thanksgiving Day 1909, and placed under the supervision of a political club, the Benevolent Order of Peerless Knights, Othello Lodge No. 1.

But it turned out that neither prison nor benevolent knights could change Shelton. On January 26, 1911, he pistol-whipped a St. Louis man in his home over a $60 debt. Shelton, ordered back to prison for five years, had come down with tuberculosis and was a skeletal 102 pounds by the time he was locked up that May. Democratic ward heelers pleaded for a mercy release, and the governor ordered him freed.

But Missouri Attorney General Elliott Major objected to the parole, and Stack Lee Shelton, not yet fifty, died in prison on March 11, 1912, before the order could be carried out. He died broke and was buried without ceremony at Greenwood Cemetery in St. Louis County. His nickname survives him in song.

CHAPTER 2

The Hard Luck of Cockeyed Cook

Billy Cook, standing on the shoulder of westbound Route 66 near Tulsa, Oklahoma, stuck out a thumb and tried to look respectable. It wasn't easy.

Although he had a delicate build at 5-foot-6 and 145 pounds, Cook had a dead-ender's mien. He wore a stained leather jacket and dungarees. One hand bore the prototypical self-inflicted prison tattoo: HARD LUCK, in two tiers across the backs of his left fingers. His chin was blotched with volcanic pimples, his teeth were prematurely rotten, and his left eye drooped but never quite managed to close completely—the result of a botched childhood operation to remove a congenital growth from that eyelid. The bad eye had stuck him with a nickname that became a sort of manifest destiny: Cockeyed Cook. Men called cockeyed become felons, not bank presidents.

Soon enough on that December day in 1950, a blue 1949 Chevrolet sedan with the Illinois license plate 233 520 rumbled to a stop just beyond Cook's thumb. Behind the wheel was Carl Mosser, thirty-three, an Illinois farmer. The car was crammed with his family: his wife Thelma, twenty-nine; and their children Ronnie, seven; Gary, five; and Pammy, three. The family's pet terrier yapped in the rear window.

The Mossers were nearly halfway through a 1,200-mile journey on Route 66—which had gained vacation fame a few years earlier thanks to Nat King Cole's hit song—from their rented farm in Atwood, Illinois, east of Springfield, to Albuquerque, New Mexico, where they planned to celebrate the holidays with Carl's twin brother, Chris, an airman at Sandia, the nuclear weapons base.

"Engine trouble," Cook told Carl Mosser, gesturing toward a car with Texas plates parked on the shoulder. The family welcomed him inside their sedan, a gracious Christmas-season act of kindness toward a stranger on the road. It would turn out to be a good deed with horrific consequences.

Billy Cook was born in 1928 in Joplin, Missouri, the country's zinc-mining capital, in the southwest corner of the state, minutes away from both Kansas and Oklahoma and a just short drive from Arkansas. His father, Will Cook, had been a cotton sharecropper near Muskogee, Oklahoma. There he met and married Laura Steven, a divorcée with four young daughters. The fertile Laura produced four more children for her new husband—first Billy, followed by two more daughters, and then a second son. Sharecropping did not support a brood that size, so Cook changed careers, moving his family one hundred miles north to Joplin (population 50,000), a booming, bawdy mining town.

The family lived in a shack on Oliver Avenue in the Chitwood section at the north fringe of Joplin, a short walk from Smelter Hill and its labyrinth of lead and zinc mines. Will Cook was a grunt laborer, pushing heavy carts laden with slag at the Eagle-Picher lead smelter. But his employment grew sporadic as the Depression set in, and he began to wander off for days or weeks at a time. During one of his absences, in 1933, the family's hard-luck life took a dire turn when mother Laura suddenly died in bed—simply worn out, the children figured.

A few days later, a local truant officer found the eight Cook children living like animals in the cavernous foyer of an abandoned lead mine. Will Cook eventually returned and tried to reclaim his fry, but welfare authorities decided they would be better off in foster homes. Cook couldn't disagree.

While his siblings adapted well to a more traditional upbringing, Billy Cook fought relentlessly against all attempts to tame him. He threw tantrums, cussed like a drunken miner, and stole anything he could get his hands on. He wore out his tenuous welcome with one foster family after another. At age eleven, he went to live with a married older stepsister, Cecilia. Even that lasted barely a week.

A chronic truant, he quit school altogether at age twelve to dedicate himself to thievery. He wasn't very good at it. Collared repeatedly, Cook was judged incorrigible and sent away for a year to the Missouri Training School for Boys in Boonville. The various rehabilitation methods used at Boonville—from corporal punishment to behavioral incentives to modern psychiatry—became secondary to the infamous education-by-osmosis at juvenile facilities. Boys traded tips on how to get away with crimes, and raw juvenile delinquents were buffed into well-polished criminals. The treachery grew so grim during Cook's stay that state policemen were called in to take over the institution from the welfare-minded mollycoddlers who were allowing the boys to run roughshod.

Not surprisingly, his year behind bars did nothing to rehabilitate Billy Cook. A week after he was freed, he robbed a Joplin cabbie of $11 and was returned to Boonville for five more years. At age seventeen, he was transferred to adult prison, where he promptly clubbed an inmate who razzed him about his droopy eye. His incarceration was extended until age twenty-one.

At Christmastime in 1949, Billy Cook was finally a free man, after spending all of his teen years locked up. He had few prospects and no vocational training. What he had was a collection of bad jailhouse tattoos on his pale skin and a chip on his shoulder the size of a cannonball. Freedom did not suit him, as all of America would soon learn.

After his parole, Cook lived briefly with his father in Joplin. The relationship became a running argument as Will Cook pressed his son to devise a sensible plan to earn a living. He later said his son was fixated on "easy dough."

"You've got to take it the hard way," Billy Cook said. "I'm going to live by the gun and roam."

Cook soon was roaming west toward California, like so many Americans. He made his way by thumb to Los Angeles. He stuck around long enough to see the Pacific Ocean, then hitchhiked back east on the old Atlantic and Pacific Highway until he landed, hungry and tired, in Blythe, a California desert town on the Colorado River opposite Arizona. Cook took a job in Blythe as a dishwasher at a café, and he slept in a cheap room in an adjacent motel. He worked a few weeks, earned a hundred bucks, then disappeared on Christmas Eve 1950. A couple of days later, he showed up in El Paso, Texas, six hundred miles east on the Atlantic-Pacific route. There he bought a .38-caliber pistol. He was about to fulfill his promise to his father.

After dark on December 29, a Texas mechanic named Lee Archer, fifty-six, stopped to pick up the hitchhiking Billy Cook near Lubbock, Texas. Archer drove north to Amarillo, then east on Route 66 into Oklahoma. At some point that night, Cook pulled his gun and forced Archer into the car trunk, after relieving him of $100. The mechanic used a jack handle to jimmy the trunk open, and he jumped out and ran like the dickens when Cook slowed for a traffic light.

Cook continued east on Route 66 across Oklahoma until the car ran out of gas near Tulsa. That is where the Good Samaritan Mossers came to his aid.

The young hitchhiker stifled car-trip chitchat by brandishing his pistol soon after taking refuge in the Mosser car. Facing the gun muzzle and following orders, Carl Mosser turned off Route 66 at Oklahoma City and drove south to Wichita Falls, Texas. With the children hungry and the Chevy low on gas, Mosser pulled into a filling station there. Cook asked E. O. Cornwall, the geriatric attendant, to fill the tank and fetch a hunk of bologna and potato chips for the kids. Cornwall replied that they'd have to get their own food, so Cook and Carl Mosser walked inside the station. When Cornwall followed them in, Mosser tried to wrestle the gun away from Cook. "Help me!" Mosser hollered at Cornwall. "He's going to kill me and take my wife! He's got us kidnapped!"

But the confused codger thought he was being drawn into a robbery scam. Cornwall pulled his own gun and ordered the men to get in their car and leave. The poor father faced a Hobson's choice: Cornwall's pistol or Cook's. The men returned to the car and drove off. Cornwall had second thoughts and followed briefly in his truck. He turned back when Cook pinged a couple of shots in his direction.

Inside the car, a seething Cook threatened to shoot Mosser and his wife. When the children cried in terror, he quieted them by promising to release everyone safely—eventually. Over the ensuing three days, he took the family on a two thousand-mile, out-and-back trip through the Southwest. They traveled across west Texas to Carlsbad, in southeastern New Mexico, within 275 miles of Albuquerque, the family's original destination. Cook got spooked by a police car in New Mexico and ordered Mosser to double back east, and they crossed the full six hundred-mile breadth of south Texas to Houston. From there they turned north and worked another six hundred miles along the Louisiana and Arkansas borders toward Cook's home turf of Joplin.

The poor Mosser family spent seventy-two hours under Cockeyed Cook's gun, including New Year's Eve 1950, and January 1, 1951. Just after midnight on January 2, Cook ordered Carl Mosser to pull the car into a farm field on the outskirts of Joplin. He told the family he was going to tie them up and leave them unharmed in the field to give him time to get away. Cook made sturdy bindings by cutting strips of cloth from clothing he took from their suitcases. He bound and gagged the parents. The children's wrists were tied with bright yellow cord he cut from the Hopalong Cassidy cowboy hats the boys had been given for Christmas.

Cook lied. He later explained that the women and children began wailing—or that he saw a police car go by and panicked. Who knows what really touched him off? He began firing at his hostages, cowered together inside the car, and didn't stop until everyone was dead, including the dog. Pammy, the toddler, was shot through the heart. The father got a bullet in the head. Little Ronnie took three bullets. The carnage lasted less than a minute, including time for Cook to reload. He pushed the bodies aside, got behind the wheel, and continued into Joplin. At 3 A.M., he quietly rolled the Chevy to the mouth of a mine shaft in his old Chitwood neighborhood. One by one, he pulled the corpses from the car and dumped them down into the darkness, where they tumbled to rest atop one another. He then split, fleeing west—once again on Route 66—until he got to Tulsa at an inopportune time.

"I arrived in the morning as people were going to work," Cook later told police. "I was excited and didn't want to be seen with all that blood in the car. I swung off on a side street and headed west on a dirt road. I slid into a muddy ditch and had to leave the car."

Hours after Cook walked away, a Tulsa cop arrived on the scene of what he thought was a routine wreck. But when he peered through the windows, he saw a murder scene—the upholstery, door panels, and floorboards punctured with bullet holes and awash in crimson. The Mossers had been reported missing when they failed to show in Albuquerque, and now Oklahoma cops suddenly had vivid evidence that the vacationing family had been slaughtered.

By the time police discovered the car, Cockeyed Cook had boarded a Greyhound in Tulsa and was bound for points west. By then, police knew his name. He had left a canvas bag of clothing in the Texas mechanic's sedan that he abandoned before the Mossers picked him up. Inside the bag, Oklahoma police found a receipt from the El Paso gun shop where Cook bought the pistol, and the shop was able to provide his name and the address he gave, the motel in Blythe, California.

Cook was further identified through Missouri prison records, and a few eyewitnesses—including Cornwall, the Wichita Falls filling station attendant—offered shreds of evidence that led police to the conclusion that the same ex-con who kidnapped the mechanic had kidnapped and killed the Illinois farm family. On January 3, a nationwide law enforcement bulletin was issued for his apprehension. The FBI made him America's Public Enemy Number 1.

The presumed murders of the Mosser family, whose bodies would not be found for nearly two weeks, made the hunt for Cockeyed Cook front-page news across the country. Thousands of law enforcers, from legitimate cops to game wardens to tin-star special deputies, eagerly joined the manhunt, and dozens of fatuous sightings were reported in a two thousand-mile arc from Minnesota to California. Despite scores of roadblocks, Cook managed to make his way unimpeded back to Blythe.

On January 6, sheriff's deputy Homer Waldrip got a hunch to visit the old Blythe motor court where Cook had briefly lived. He was in the process of knocking at each room when Cook suddenly flung open a door, snatched Waldrip's revolver, led him to his patrol car, and ordered the deputy to drive them west. Waldrip said Cook bragged about murdering the Mosser family, and the deputy assumed he was about to meet the same fate when Cook ordered him to stop in the desert thirty-five miles from Blythe. But Cook allowed Waldrip to run free for reasons unexplained, then squealed away in his patrol car. Seven miles up the road, he used the siren to pull over a 1947 Buick driven by Robert Dewey, a vacationing Seattle salesman. He abandoned the patrol car, shot and killed Dewey, dumped his body, then fled south toward Mexico, just an hour's drive away.

Dewey's Buick was found discarded beside the road fifty miles into Mexico, on Baja California. There, Cook used his gun to kidnap two more men, James Burke and Forrest Damron, hobby prospectors from the border town of El Centro, California, who were on a gold-hunting adventure in Mexico. As he made his way south down the Baja peninsula, a gun leveled on his two latest hostages, Cockeyed Cook might have imagined that he was home free.

Back in Oklahoma, authorities and volunteers relentlessly scoured the Tulsa area for the bodies of the Mosser family. But a sharp Joplin cop, Walter Gamble, got a hunch they were looking in the wrong place. A forensic investigation of the Mosser car had turned up traces of shale, the sedimentary rock common to the southwest Missouri mining region. On a hunch, Gamble and his colleagues began checking pits and shafts in Cook's old Joplin haunts.

Late on the morning of January 15, someone finally shone a flashlight down the right shaft. Thirty feet down lay the wrecked bodies of the Mossers, piled helter-skelter atop crisscrossed timbers in the flooded mine. Joplin firemen were lowered into the mine by cables to retrieve the grim cargo. The first body they raised was Pammy, the youngest victim. Next came Gary, Ronnie, mother Thelma and, finally, Carl Mosser. The family was reassembled side-by-side on a tarp laid out near the mine. Firemen and hundreds of spectators, including news photographers from across the country, wept at the sight. In Ronnie's trouser pocket, police found the boy's Hopalong Cassidy wallet. Cockeyed Cook had taken every penny from Carl and Thelma Mosser. But little Ronnie didn't give up his loot to the pitiless killer. His wallet contained $1.75—a buck, six dimes, and fifteen pennies.

That same morning, Francisco Morales, police chief for the vast state of Tijuana, Mexico, fielded a call from a subordinate in Santa Rosalia, six hundred miles south of the border. The underling told Morales that Cook and his captives had been spotted in Santa Rosalia, a fishing village on the Gulf of California. Morales scrambled to an airplane and hurried there. The local *policia* led the chief to a restaurant where the visiting Americans had been quietly tailed. Morales walked up to Cook's table and put a gun to his ear.

Playing against type, Cook surrendered. He was disarmed, and his captives were freed. Morales and his quarry returned by plane to

Tijuana, and the hero chief turned over Cook to U.S. authorities at the border after he was dismissed from the country as undesirable. Asked by an American cop why he had done it, Cook is said to have replied, "I hate everybody's guts, and everybody hates mine."

On January 21, Cook was returned to Oklahoma, where he faced federal kidnapping and murder charges—a conviction that since passage of the Lindbergh Law in 1932 had meant a sure penalty of death.

First came the mandatory psychiatric examination. Four different shrinks put a candle to Cook's ear; three decided he was sane enough to stand trial. The fourth wasn't so sure. The point became moot on March 13 when U.S. District Court Judge Stephen Chandler surprised everyone by agreeing to accept a guilty plea from Cook. The judge rejected a death sentence and gave him the 1951 equivalent of life without parole—five consecutive sixty-year terms, for a total of three hundred years. The public was outraged, but no more than the federal prosecutor, Thomas Shelton.

"The godamnedest travesty of justice ever," Shelton said. "If ever a crime deserved the death penalty, this is it! I want the court and society and the public to know where law enforcement stands."

Minutes after the sentence was announced, the U.S. Justice Department—with encouragement from FBI Director J. Edgar Hoover—announced that it would turn Cockeyed Cook over to District Attorney Don Bitler in Imperial County, California, who was eager to prosecute him for the murder of Robert Dewey, the Seattle salesman.

By the opening day of the state trial in the fall of 1951, the nation all but demanded lethal comeuppance for Cook. The trial seemed a pre–death sentence formality. A shrink testified Cook was sane, but "lacking any human compassion, feeling or sentiment." The jury took fifty minutes to convict Cook, who sat through the proceedings wearing a smirk. His smiled tightened when Superior Court Judge Luray Mouser passed sentence: death. America got its wish.

Defense Attorney John Connolly pressed a series of appeals centered on the idea that Cook was "obviously insane." His efforts failed, and Billy Cook faced his end on December 12, 1952, still just twenty-three years old.

He was a hard case to the end, refusing comfort from clergymen and waving off news scribes hoping for a Death Row exclusive. He ate a last supper of fried chicken, French fries, peas, and pumpkin pie on December 11. The following morning, he strode wordlessly past witnesses and was strapped into the death chair in the San Quentin prison gas chamber, freshly painted a sickly industrial green. The door was sealed just after 10 A.M. A cloud of deadly cyanide fumes engulfed the spree killer, and he departed life with three last gasps. Afterwards, Harley Teets, San Quentin's legendary warden, spoke a dozen words that serve as an apt epitaph for Cock-eyed Cook. "He was the most completely alone young man I have ever encountered," Teets said.

One final indignity lay ahead in the story of Billy Cook's wasted life, thanks to a huckster Oklahoma mortician named Glen Boydstun. He ran a funeral home in Comanche, a drowsy cotton town ninety miles south of Oklahoma City, near the Texas border. Boydstun was old enough to recall Oklahoma's long history with a morose form of Old West capitalism. Okies had always loved to ogle the bullet-ventilated bodies of outlaws, and they didn't mind paying a nickel or better to do so. In 1934, the body of Pretty Boy Floyd drew as many as forty thousand morbid tourists to a funeral home in Sallisaw, Oklahoma, on the Arkansas border near Fort Smith. The following year, the bodies of Ma and Fred Barker drew throngs to tiny Welch, Oklahoma, an hour from Joplin.

Fifteen years later, the bald, portly Boydstun decided to try his luck at a death display of Cockeyed Cook in Comanche—despite the fact that the town had absolutely nothing to do with Cook or his crimes. Boydstun contacted Will Cook in Joplin and disingenuously intoned that he would be willing to foot the bill for a proper burial for his wayward son. Will Cook signed his permission for Boydstun to claim the body at San Quentin, and the mortician pointed his hearse toward California. Three days after the execution, Cook's corpse—outfitted in a suit and tie—was on public display in Comanche. Boydstun was dissatisfied with the initial day's box-office proceeds, so he added loudspeakers outside the mortuary to entice customers, like a sideshow barker, to see "the last American desperado."

Thousands came on the second day, including busloads of schoolchildren. In all, as many as twelve thousand people eyed the body before Cook's siblings had had enough. They hired a lawyer, wrestled their brother's corpse away from Boydstun, and returned it to Joplin. The mortician grumbled, "The deal backfired on me."

Billy Cook's body was escorted by his older sisters one final time east along Route 66 and back into Joplin on December 21, 1952, the shortest day of the year. It was dark by the time the entourage made its way through the old Chitwood section, past mine fields and chat piles of tailings, then north a couple of miles to Peace Church Cemetery, a century-old Baptist graveyard. By flashlight, Cook's siblings saw to it that Billy was lowered six feet under. His brief, peripatetic life was over—mercifully, perhaps, for all concerned.

CHAPTER 3

The Small Town
That Had Enough

The remains of Ken Rex McElroy, Missouri's most infamous modern rogue, lie six feet under at Memorial Park cemetery in St. Joseph, in a grave thirty paces from a relief sculpture of the Last Supper.

Over the years, the grass has encroached on his flat tombstone, obscuring a line of script at the bottom of the marker. Push aside the greenery and you can make out the three adjectives his kin used to memorialize their "Beloved Ken": BRAVE, FEARLESS, AND COMPASSIONATE.

The people of Skidmore, Missouri, fifty miles north of St. Joe, tended to use less heroic words to describe McElroy. He was a bully, they said. A thief. A coward. An intimidator of the weak and vulnerable. A stalker. A statutory rapist. McElroy, a fleshy man with an Elvis-inspired pompadour dyed as black as crow feathers, was Skidmore's scourge. He broke laws and got away with it, over and over and over again. He seemed to be a Teflon-coated hick—until a sweltering summer morning in 1981, when the town finally had had enough.

A crowd surrounded McElroy's Chevy pickup, parked outside the D&G Tavern on Skidmore's main street. At least two people fired gunshots into the cab of the truck, and Ken Rex McElroy was killed—yes, in broad daylight—in an act of vigilante justice that focused klieg lights on the northwest Missouri hamlet. The killers have never been identified, despite the protracted efforts of local, state, and federal law enforcers to coax an informant from the crowd of witnesses.

Skidmore has kept its secret for thirty years and counting. But a visit to the town left me wondering whether it might have doomed itself in the process. In 1981, it was a robust farming hub. Today, it seems on the verge of slipping into oblivion—which might suit its dwindling citizenry, who have grown increasingly weary and wary of scrutiny from outsiders.

The town lies on a rise above a gentle, sweeping bend in the sandy Nodaway River. Rolling fields of corn and soybeans press against the village from all directions. The official population count of 342 seems blindly optimistic. There are nearly as many vacant houses as occupied ones in the eight-block checkerboard of streets. Yards are decorated with rusting tractor wheels, old plows, and other farm implements from yesteryear. You can buy a fixer-upper there for less than $10,000—and real estate agents in Maryville, a college town fourteen miles away, add that everything in Skidmore is negotiable. Owners have simply abandoned a number of dwellings, leaving them to tumble down.

The bank, the grocery store, and the gas station are gone. So is the D&G Tavern. When the only café in town closed in 2010, a local agri-businessman with a few bucks to spare opened a chat-'n'-chew bar and cafe he named the Outcast, an inside joke. But even this bit of good news from Skidmore was presented with a negative nudge. "There is no nice way to say it," began a story about the new establishment in the *Maryville Daily Forum*. "Downtown Skidmore is in trouble."

What's left in town are a couple of churches, a grain elevator, an automotive repair shop, and the Outcast. Not so long ago, the federal government gave Skidmore a new post office—the only thing in town that seems fresh. Walk around the disintegrating hamlet and you understand that McElroy may have gotten the last laugh on Skidmore. It is going to seed.

The little town may have no future. But it will always have a past, thanks to McElroy. He was born in 1934, the next-to-last of sixteen children of a tenant-farming couple who migrated during the Depression years from one failed farm to the next in the American breadbasket. The McElroy clan happened to alight at a leased farm outside Skidmore, and Ken took root there.

He was the sort of boy who could not be bothered with school, and he dropped out before gaining full literacy. As a teenager he was known as a first-rate coon hunter, tailing his hounds with a .22 rifle as they tracked raccoons after dark along tree-lined creeks. This was not merely sport. Coon hunting is a venerable hillbilly trade, and he made walking-around money by skinning the animals and selling the pelts, earning a few bucks apiece in bad years, ten dollars or more in good years.

It turned out that after-hours work suited McElroy. He rarely had a legitimate job, yet he drove new pickup trucks and seemed to have ample cash to indulge the various young women and teenagers he ran about with. McElroy prowled the region during the day, making note of anything of value that wasn't locked up. He then returned at night to scoop up his quarry—feed corn, gasoline, booze, furniture, and anything else he could fence in Kansas City or St. Joseph. He became an ace at rustling, herding unbranded livestock onto a trailer and then selling them for 50 cents on the dollar at crooked slaughterhouses or livestock barns.

Good citizens came to understand that McElroy was dishonest, and they assumed he would get his comeuppance from the criminal justice system, sooner or later. After all, doesn't the bad guy always lose in America? Maybe not.

It was his way with women—or nubile girls—that began to make it seem as though Ken McElroy had somehow managed to inoculate himself against the laws that govern the rest of us. McElroy married at age eighteen, in 1952, but his wedding band proved irrelevant. He pursued the region's adolescent girls with a lusty gusto, often hanging out at school playgrounds or befriending adolescent boys to gain entrée to their female peers. His modus operandi was to focus his bullish blandishments on girls from poor, unsophisticated families, courting them with cheap jewelry and backroad rides in his pickup.

McElroy divorced his wife after a few years and married a fifteen-year-old girl named Sharon, who was pregnant with his child. He then began pursuing a thirteen-year-old named Sally, threatening to beat the girl and kill her father unless she acquiesced to his sexual demands. Sally moved in with Sharon and McElroy, and the two teenagers gave birth to a total of seven of McElroy's children from 1961 to 1965. The girls were pregnant simultaneously several times. In 1964, with Sharon pregnant again and both young women caring for newborns, McElroy abandoned them and took up housekeeping with Alice, a fifteen-year-old from St. Joseph. As she began churning out more McElroy fry, Alice was joined in the bedroom and maternity ward by Marcia, yet another of McElroy's child-lovers.

What did these girls see in him? A clenched fist, more than anything. He beat every woman he was intimate with, and one would later tell author Harry N. MacLean that McElroy's sex was violent and demeaning. His flabby flesh was marred by a collection of awful tattoos: Mom, Ken, Love, a dagger. His belly lapped over his belt, and his wide-set eyes were crowned by a beetle brow. He accentuated a vague resemblance to Elvis by growing mutton-chop sideburns. And in an odd bit of vanity for a fat redneck, he dyed his hair an inky black. It could not have been an attractive portrait of a lover for a pubescent girl. But one teenager after another found herself the target of McElroy's groping mitts.

Trena McCloud was twelve years old, a blonde eighth-grader, when she became the focus of McElroy's leer. He was pushing middle age, had fathered ten children, and already had two young women, Alice and Marcia, sharing his bedroom. McElroy barely bothered trying to hide his latest rapacious child romance, and the relationship became an open secret in town. Half the kids in Trena's class knew all about it, including the name of the St. Joseph motel where McElroy took the child for sex. The year was 1972—not exactly the dark ages. Yet no authority figure stepped forward to challenge a serial statutory rapist who by then had preyed on at least five underage girls. Local school officials would later admit that they were aware of rumors about McElroy's relationship with Trena McCloud but had failed to conduct a responsible investigation.

Trena, still just fourteen, turned up pregnant in ninth grade. She dropped out and moved in with McElroy and Alice, replacing Marcia in the harem. Neither girl was happy with this life, which featured regular beatings by their keeper. Two weeks after Trena gave birth, she and Alice fled with their children to the home of Trena's mother. McElroy brought them back home at gunpoint. He beat them savagely, subjected them to sexual torture, and then burned down the mother's house. As a coup de grâce, he shot the woman's dog.

Intercession finally arrived—not from police, not from school, not even from Trena's mother. A conscientious pediatrician in nearby Mound City, Missouri, drew the story out of the terrified teenager during a checkup on her infant. The doctor reached out to proper authorities—finally. The baby and Trena were placed in a foster home safe house in Maryville, and in June 1973 McElroy was charged with arson, rape, and assault.

A year earlier, McElroy had been arrested on a felony theft charge for stealing cattle. He hired Richard McFadin, a criminal defense lawyer from Kansas City, one hundred miles away. McFadin got him off the hook, and the case began a long, mutually beneficial relationship for both men. "Best client I ever had," McFadin liked to say of McElroy. "Paid in cash and kept coming back."

McFadin's standing fee for McElroy was $5,000 per felony, so his Skidmore client arrived with a bag of $15,000 in cash after he was released on bail following the arson rampage. McFadin advised McElroy that the charges would be hard to beat if Trena testified against him. So McElroy went to work on the girl, using a stalking tactic that would become part of his standard repertoire. McElroy began sitting in his truck outside the Maryville safe house, staring at the windows. The foster family called police, but they were told that McElroy had a legal right to sit and stare. He also began making intimidating calls to the foster mother, suggesting a "girl for girl" trade—her own child for Trena.

It is unfathomable that such intimidation of witnesses in a criminal case could happen, even in 1973. But McElroy seemed immune to the rules of civilized society. It appeared that Missouri authorities feared him for reasons never explained. And the absurdities grew deeper when it occurred to McElroy and McFadin that a sure way to beat the felony rap was for the accused to marry the accuser.

In 1974, Trena and the baby left the foster home and moved in with her grandmother. McElroy's truck soon was showing up there. McElroy was still married to his second wife, Sharon. She dutifully showed up at McFadin's office seeking a divorce. With that quickly accomplished, there was one other catch. Trena was still just fifteen, so her mother had to authorize the marriage. Having already been burned out of one house, she acquiesced. A rural Missouri judge performed the ceremony on the same day that Trena's mother signed the authorization. Attorney McFadin was the witness.

The marriage eliminated Trena as a witness. The prosecutor could have taken the hard way and pressed the case, even without Trena. But he chose to take the easy way and dismissed the charges. Incredibly, McElroy, Trena, and Alice resumed their life together. Once again, the good people of Skidmore were left to wonder over their invincible neighbor. But his days were numbered.

On July 27, 1976, a Skidmore farmer named Romaine Henry, forty-one, heard gunshots near his farmhouse. He investigated and found McElroy standing on the road holding a shotgun. McElroy opened the passenger door of Henry's truck, pointed the gun at him and growled, "Were you the dirty son of a bitch over at my place in a white Pontiac?" McElroy fired twice, hitting Henry in the torso and head with buckshot. The injured farmer managed to speed away, and McElroy was arrested and charged with assault. He called upon McFadin in Kansas City and again employed his intimidation routine. Henry said McElroy parked outside or slow-rolled past his home more than one hundred times in the months after the shooting. Henry complained, but the county sheriff said he could do nothing.

At trial, McFadin outmaneuvered a young prosecutor in her first serious felony trial. The jury voted to acquit, siding with McElroy over the word of a victim who looked his attacker in the eye from five feet away. The gossip around Skidmore was that the backstory to the shooting concerned "a woman." Henry, married with children, was not seen as innocent. So Skidmore let it be. But in retrospect, the arc of one event to the next in McElroy's life couldn't be clearer.

The endgame for McElroy sprang from a tiff on April 25, 1980, when several of his children stopped at Skidmore's B&B grocery for candy. The store was owned by Bo and Lois Bowenkamp. Bo, a gangly 6-foot-5, was a reserved fellow who had grown up with German immigrant parents on an Iowa farm an hour's drive north of Skidmore. Bowenkamp was newly divorced in 1960 when he met Lois, a divorcée waitress in Shenandoah, Iowa. Feisty and outspoken, she was twenty years younger than he was. The couple moved to nearby Plattsmouth, Nebraska, where Bowenkamp worked as a carpenter. In 1972, with Bo about ready to retire, they moved to Lois's hometown of Skidmore. They bought the local grocery store in 1977. Bo manned the meat counter while Lois worked the register.

On that spring afternoon in 1980, one of the younger McElroy children left the store crying, and an older half-sister told Trena McElroy that Lois Bowenkamp had accused the child of shoplifting. Ken McElroy's pickup squealed to a stop outside the store twenty minutes later. He and Trena rushed inside and cussed Lois

Bowenkamp, with Trena vowing to "whip your ass." Lois ordered them out of the store and announced they were barred from doing business there.

By that evening, McElroy had resorted to his old tricks: stalking and intimidation. He sat in his truck outside the store and stared. When the Bowenkamps went home, McElroy followed in his truck, slowly cruising past the Bowenkamp place over and over. Threatening phone calls soon followed. Lois Bowenkamp reported these incidents to the authorities, but she got the sheriff department's usual know-nothing reply: Ken McElroy has a legal right to stare.

After dark on May 29, a month after the candy dispute, Lois Bowenkamp watched through a window as McElroy stood on the road outside, pointed a shotgun at her house, raised the barrel slightly, and fired two shots. Thirty minutes later, he drove by again and fired another shot. Lois Bowenkamp drove to Maryville to file a report with the Nodaway County Sheriff's Office. Sheriff Roger Cronk promised he would report the incident to the county prosecutor, and he added the absurd proviso that Lois should keep an eye on McElroy. How could she not? He was stalking her at work and at home. Two nights later, McElroy again fired his shotgun outside the Bowenkamp home. The Bowenkamps were being harassed, intimidated, threatened, and even assaulted, according to even the most uninformed reading of Missouri law. For reasons never adequately explained, Sheriff Cronk did not file that report, did not speak with McElroy, and did not seek other witnesses. He did nothing. Under assault from a bully and hunkered down in their home, Bo and Lois Bowenkamp must have felt utterly alone.

On July 8, 1980, Bo Bowenkamp waited after-hours at the grocery store for an air-conditioner repairman. McElroy suddenly materialized at the back door and pointed a shotgun at him. As Bowenkamp, nearly seventy years old, turned to run, McElroy touched off a blast that hit the grocer in the head and torso. The old man fell in a heap. A boy who heard the shot ran toward the store and found Bowenkamp awash in blood. "Who did it?" the first cop on the scene asked. Bowenkamp replied, "Ken McElroy."

State police arrested McElroy that night. He denied everything, phoned his Kansas City lawyer, and was out on bond the next morning. That night, he and Trena were back in the D&G Tavern, drinking beers and laughing about the shooting.

Bo Bowenkamp spent ten days in the hospital but survived. McElroy claimed that the old man had menaced him with a knife and that he fired in self-defense. Potential witnesses against him began receiving his customary threats, including the part-time town marshal, David Dunbar. When Dunbar said he might have to testify against him, McElroy replied, "I'll kill anybody who would put me in jail." Dunbar said McElroy then pointed a shotgun at him. He reported the incident to the sheriff, who replied, by rote: nothing we can do. Dunbar resigned. McElroy then began slow-rolling his truck past the home of another potential witness, Richard Stratton, the state trooper who had arrested him. Lois Bowenkamp might have been speaking for all of them, for all of Skidmore, when she sent a letter to Missouri's governor, pleading for intervention. She wrote, "Are we to live in fear for the rest of our lives?"

After a year of legal maneuvering by attorney McFadin, McElroy's felony assault trial began on June 25, 1981. It was a simple case of one man's story against another's. Bowenkamp said McElroy shot him in an unprovoked attack following months of intimidation. McElroy said he fired after Bowenkamp menaced him with a knife. The primary witnesses were the two men. Prosecutor David Baird, twenty-seven, just three years out of law school, presented a competent case. McFadin pinned his hopes on a witness he dredged up—a friend of McElroy—who claimed she was driving by and saw Bowenkamp lunge at McElroy.

Inside the jury room, a quick first vote established that jurors wished to convict McElroy of assault. But to what degree? If they convicted him of first-degree assault, he could have faced up to life in prison. But under state law, the jury was not informed of McElroy's rap sheet of twenty criminal charges over the years because he had always evaded felony convictions. So the unaware jurors voted to convict him of second-degree assault and recommended a sentence of just two years in prison. McFadin asked that McElroy be set free while the lawyer prepared an appeal. The judge continued his bail and turned him loose.

Skidmore's scourge was down but not out.

Four days later, McElroy strode into the D&G Tavern armed with an M-1 assault rifle equipped with a bayonet. As he sat at the bar swigging beers, he told the bartender and a handful of customers that he planned to use the gun to finish off Bo Bowenkamp, and then carve him up like a turkey with the bayonet. Customers reported the threat to prosecutor Baird, who began proceedings to revoke McElroy's bail. A hearing was set for July 10, and dozens of Skidmore citizens planned to meet at the American Legion Hall that morning to travel to the courthouse as a group to oppose the bully's continued freedom. The hearing was postponed ten days at the eleventh hour, but the get-together at the Legion went on that morning nonetheless, attended by sixty men and a handful of women. It became a McElroy gripe session, and the group asked Sheriff Danny Estes to drive over from Maryville to advise them about how they could protect themselves against McElroy. Estes suggested that townspeople should keep an eye on McElroy. Someone at the meeting said, "But isn't that your job, sheriff?"

As Estes left, word arrived at the Legion that McElroy was in town. He had parked his shiny new Chevy Silverado on Main Street and ambled inside the D&G with Trena for a redneck breakfast of a beer, a Camel cigarette, and a couple of Rolaids. McElroy wanted everyone in town to know that he knew they were talking about him.

The Legion crowd gravitated toward the D&G. Some stayed outside, and some went in for a stare-down with McElroy. The bully ordered a six-pack to go, and he and Trena walked outside and climbed into the Silverado. Witnesses said he sat in the cab and smiled defiantly, then pulled a Camel from his new pack and put it between his lips. Before he had a chance to light it, two rifle shots rang out from the left, followed by four more the rear. Glass shattered in the driver's door and at the back of the cab. The loud reports sent the crowd diving for cover. Trena emerged from the passenger side, splattered with blood and screaming. Someone in the bar called for help, and Sheriff Estes, who was headed back to Maryville, did a U-turn toward Skidmore. He found McElroy dead, hit with at least one .22-caliber slug and another from an 8mm rifle. There were as many as thirty-five witnesses, but each of them had lockjaw by the time Estes arrived, no more than fifteen minutes after the shooting. Nobody saw a thing.

The vigilante killing and cover-up was big national news, and the attention brought pressure to bear on law enforcers to solve the real-life whodunit. A task force of two dozen officers from six Missouri law enforcement agencies applied pressure to the witnesses, pleading and then threatening. It didn't work. They set up a telephone tip line. No one called it but reporters. Nodaway County prosecutor Baird convened a coroner's inquest. Six jurors heard evidence from cops, Trena McElroy, and several men who were at the scene, including postmaster Jim Hartman, the village mayor, and Red Smith, bartender at the D&G. The inquest led to an obvious conclusion: that McElroy "had died from bullets fired by a person or persons unknown." A state grand jury was impaneled, meeting fifteen times over five weeks. Jurors heard from Del Clement, a young farmer and son of an owner of the D&G Tavern. Trena McElroy had fingered him as one of the men holding a gun after the shooting. But no witness would corroborate her testimony, and the state grand jury also voted against indictments. Next came an FBI investigation. Evidence was presented to a federal grand jury in the spring of 1982, but it ended with the same result: no charges.

In 1984, attorney McFadin filed a $5 million wrongful death civil lawsuit on behalf of Trena McElroy against Sheriff Estes, Skidmore mayor Steve Peter, and Del Clement. The defendants settled out of court for a paltry $17,600, with the county paying $12,600, Skidmore, $2,000, and Clement, $3,000. They said they paid to avoid costly legal fees, not as an admission of guilt.

After all the fruitless probing was complete, prosecutor Baird announced, "After careful consideration and evaluation, I have determined that there is not current sufficient evidence with which to establish guilt beyond a reasonable doubt." And there the murder investigation sits, three decades along, after two books, a film, and millions of words tapped out by journalists and other busybodies. Writers have described the case as Skidmore's "nightmare that won't go away" and "a scab that is continually picked." The principal figures in the murder have gradually died, including Bo and Lois Bowenkamp and Del Clement. Trena McElroy remarried and moved away. The law enforcers involved are all retired, as is defense attorney McFadin, well into his eighties. In 2010, Baird was voted out of office after thirty years. The McElroy case was a popular subject in his exit interviews with the press. He repeated the position he has maintained over the years: that only a handful of people—not thirty-five—know the identities of the shooters that day.

A few years back, I reached out to Lois Bowenkamp's daughters, Joyce Monty and Cheryl Huston, to talk about the case. Huston was still living in the region, and Monty had spent much of her adult life in Oklahoma. Their answers to my questions always came back around to one theme: justice.

"If the law and courts had done what needed to be done to stop that man years before 1980 and 1981 came around, none of any of it would have happened," said Monty. "How did one man manage to bully and terrorize his way to such a point that a judge wouldn't lock him up and throw the key away for the good of the community? Part of the answer is a problem that still haunts the justice system: The law of the land bends over backwards to insure the rights of the criminals, not their victims. Period."

Her sister had a slightly different take.

"I believe wholeheartedly that the criminal justice system not only let us down," Huston said, "but let the McElroy family down as well."

The case did leave a criminal justice legacy in that it helped spur the victim's rights movement, prompting law enforcers to reexamine their treatment of traditionally low-priority crimes such as stalking, harassment, and threats.

The Bowenkamp daughters—like Skidmore itself—are filled with regrets about the McElroy saga. Monty said she regretted not having been more assertive in demanding protection for her parents from the preposterously passive county sheriff. Huston, beset with lingering psychological problems over the shooting and aftermath, said she rued cooperating with writers, who left her feeling used and abandoned.

Joyce Monty told me that she hoped the shooters are never identified, in part because they would then be subjected to the same justice system that failed her family. "That is one killing that needs to be left unresolved," she said.

But what about Skidmore, branded forever as the vigilante town?

"If somebody had been charged and convicted, there would have been a sense of closure," Skidmore mayor Debbie Abrams told a journalist not long ago. "As long as this town stands and probably even after it's gone, we will always be known for what happened here that day."

I asked Joyce Monty to describe Skidmore before the McElroy mess. Without meaning to be ironic, she replied, "Skidmore was a town that minded its own business."

CHAPTER 4
Look Out for the Cheater

On April 10, 1987, a crew of law enforcers gathered in the back-yard of a suburban home on Gutermuth Road in St. Charles County, Missouri, west of St. Louis. They were looking for the body of a man who had been missing for more than three years, and they had reason to believe they could find it there, at the former home of an electrician known as Big Jim Williams.

Deputies edged aside an oversized leaden planter that had been strategically positioned over the lid of a rainwater cistern. They unfastened the heavy cover, and someone aimed a flashlight into the black water below. A lifeless human form was floating inside, just as they expected.

Over the next several hours, the body was carefully removed. It was a good-looking man in his late thirties, dressed in a jogging suit. He had been trussed up and shot squarely in the back. Someone had gone through the bother of weighing down the corpse with concrete blocks. Investigators carefully raked through the cistern and found three spent shells from a .410 shotgun. They also dredged up a plastic bag containing a collection of credit cards and a Missouri driver's license. The photo on the license matched the face in the cistern. He was Walter Notheis Jr. Around St. Louis, Notheis was not a nobody. And the story of how this somebody ended up dead is a classic true-crime tale of lust, greed, and a deadly love triangle— or more accurately, a love quadrangle.

Two decades earlier, in 1966, rock n' roll disc jockeys had begun spinning a catchy single by a clean-cut St. Louis combo called Bob Kuban and the In-Men. This was no garage band. It was an eight-piece ensemble with a horn section featuring a trombone, trumpet, and saxophone. Most of the In-Men studied music in college, and a couple of them were music teachers. St. Louis—hometown to the likes of Scott Joplin, Clark Terry, Josephine Baker, Miles Davis, Albert King, and Chuck Berry—has always had a rich musical tradition, and the In-Men dreamed that they could be the next big thing from the Gateway City.

The last member invited into the band was the lead vocalist. He played no instrument and was not a trained musician, but he sang with soul, which fit the band. He could sing in tune, had decent range, and possessed a dynamic stage presence after several years fronting school combos. There was a downside: He had the rather uninspiring ethnic German name of Walter Notheis Jr.—not exactly Mick Jagger. He was accepted into the band but encouraged to take on a stage name. And so Sir Walter Scott was born.

The In-Men worked up a repertoire of Top-40 covers, especially horn tunes made famous by Detroit's Motown and by Stax Records, three hundred miles down the Mississippi in Memphis. The band developed a wardrobe of sharp matching suits and polished their act at Catholic school dances before graduating to legitimate gigs at the St. Louis Playboy Club and other venues in Gaslight Square, the entertainment district in the city's Central West End.

The band's manager pressed the In-Men to develop original material, and bass player Mike Krenski—the best songwriter among the eight—came up with a two-and-a-half-minute story-song with a great pop-lyric hook. Any Baby Boomer can sing along to the chorus:

Look out for the cheater
Make way for the fool-hearted clown
Look out for the cheater
He's gonna build you up just to let you down

The In-Men recorded "The Cheater" at a St. Louis studio in late 1965, and the band's manager shopped it to local radio stations. From there it went viral to stations coast to coast, the way pop songs once could. It eventually brushed up against the pop chart Top 10, and it won drummer Bob Kuban and his mates an appearance on *American Bandstand* on April 30, 1966. It was a golden opportunity, and the band seemed poised for stardom.

But rock n' roll has always been a racket where egos get in the way of sound decision-making. Just as they were gaining fame, the In-Men splintered in a fight over money and marquee status. Why should Kuban, the non-singing percussionist, get top billing and a bigger cut of fees and royalties? Walter Scott, the lead vocalist and frontman, reckoned that he should be the star, just as frontman Jagger was star of the Rolling Stones. So he and several other members of the In-Men split and formed a new combo: Walter Scott and the Guise. The lead vocalist had top billing, for what it was worth.

Walter Notheis Jr. was a World War II baby, born in St. Louis on February 7, 1943, the first of two sons of solid, blue-collar parents, Walter and Kay. His father spent the first three years of little Wally's life in the Navy, then had a long career operating a crane at American Car and Foundry Company, a venerable St. Louis firm that manufactured railroad cars. His mother worked in the city's vast Proctor & Gamble factory.

Walter Jr. spent his formative years in Dutchtown, one of the many largely German neighborhoods in St. Louis. He attended St. Peter and Paul grade school in Soulard, south of downtown, then went to high school nearby at St. Mary's, a Catholic school for boys. Walter cut his musical eye teeth in high school as vocalist for a teen band called the Royaltones. He met a petite brunette named Doris at a sock hop in 1959, and they were married in a Catholic ceremony four years later, a couple of weeks before Walter's twentieth birthday. The young couple soon had two sons. The second, Scotty, was born a few months after the In-Men's big date on *American Bandstand*.

But by then, Sir Walter had one foot out of the brief marriage.

Walter Scott had stars in his eyes and a lover on the side by the time he was fronting his own band. He believed he could be the next blue-eyed soul star, a la Johnny Rivers. But it turned out he was more of a Bruce Channel ("Hey! Baby"), a one-hit wonder who would never again manage to make musical magic. His band The Guise performed as five pieces, without a horn section. Their sound had nothing in common with the In-Men's hit. Instead, they tried to copy the British "Mod" sound, a la the Dave Clark Five and Herman's Hermits, with silly pop songs and heavy use of a cheesy-sounding Farfisa organ. The Guise recorded a number of originals, but they went nowhere. The group soon disbanded, and the remnants—including Sir Walter—carried on as the Kommotions, a cover band.

But even one-hit wonders can manage to make a living performing their signature tune, night after night, gig after gig, year after year. And so it was with Walter Notheis Jr. He developed an act, with dancers and backup singers, and took it on the road to resort areas—the Pennsylvania Poconos, the Catskills in New York, the Florida shuffleboard circuit, New Jersey's Atlantic City, Playboy Clubs in St. Louis, and elsewhere. He became a specialist at covering Neil Diamond hits, along with Elvis and other oldies. "The

Cheater" was always the highlight, of course. But Walter should have been more mindful of the lyrics.

Walter carved out a respectable living, driving a luxury car and residing on Lake Pershing in an upscale subdivision in St. Peters, a suburb thirty miles west of downtown St. Louis on Interstate 70. He spent much of his time on the road, living the rock 'n' roll lifestyle. This took a toll on Walter's family life.

By the time his second son was born, Walter was fooling around with a St. Louis television-station secretary named JoAnn Calcaterra—an attractive brunette, like his wife. Doris became redundant, and Walter divorced her and married JoAnn on Christmas Eve 1969. She gave birth to twins a couple of years later. But that marriage eventually became a yawner as well. Walter hooked up while on the road with one of his backup singers, Serina Michaels. They had an action-packed sex life, according to true-crime author Scottie Priesmeyer, including swinger's clubs, pornographic self-portraits, and employment of various other forms of sexual stimuli.

And it turned out that while Walter was on the road fooling around, his second wife wasn't sitting at home twiddling her thumbs.

In October 1982, a gigantic electrician named Jim Williams was hired to make a minor repair at the Notheis lake home in St. Peters. Walter was out of town, as usual, so JoAnn was home alone. She showed the electrician her problem—and then some. Williams was built like a football tight end, at 6-foot-6 and 250 pounds. It was lust at first sight.

Jim Williams, then forty-three, had grown up in Indiana and attended high school in Marion, Illinois, two hours southeast of St. Louis. In 1958, he married a Marion girl named Sharon Almaroad. After Williams served a stint in the Navy, the couple had two sons and moved into a trailer north of St. Louis, where he took a job with McDonnell Douglas and she worked as a clerk for TWA.

Williams was a talented handyman who had an odd-jobs side business for years. He eventually decided that he could earn more money as a builder and electrician, so he quit his job after eleven years with the aerospace giant. It was business that led him to JoAnn Notheis in the fall of 1982. Nine months later, in July 1983, Big Jim Williams casually mentioned to a couple of his contracting company employees that he was in the market for a subcontractor with a specific skill. "Do you guys know any hit men?" he asked.

On the rainy, windy evening of October 19, 1983, Sharon Williams left her home on Gutermuth Road in suburban St. Charles County. During a phone conversation that day, she told her mother back home in Illinois that she was going to attend the Wednesday evening service at a Baptist church in nearby Harvester, Missouri. At 7:20 that night, a couple driving on Central School Road not far from the Williams's home spotted the taillights of a Cadillac that had run down an embankment and into a ditch. The Samaritans hurried down the hill and stomped out a fire in the weeds near the car. The only occupant of the wreck was Sharon Williams. She was in a peculiar position, nearly tucked completely under the dashboard on the passenger side. The driver's door was wide open. The first rescuers found the victim gasping for air. She had a gruesome wound to the back of her head. She was rushed to a hospital—alive, but barely.

Everyone who viewed the crash scene and several of the medical personnel involved in the care of Sharon Williams seemed to agree that nothing seemed quite right about the wreck. An ambulance attendant said it appeared that someone had splashed gasoline on the victim, then left a trail of gas from the car to the weeds that the Samaritan found on fire. The position of the body was all wrong. And how does a woman suffer a severe wound to the back of her head when she drives into a ditch? Someone at the hospital phoned the St. Charles Sheriff's Department to voice concerns. They were put on terminal hold. The staffer hung up, and the hospital staff let it drop.

Sheriff's personnel at the scene figured that the woman had simply slid off the road during the rainstorm. It was an accident, they assumed. The next day, Jim Williams was informed by the hospital that Sharon had no chance of recovery. He ordered his wife of twenty-five years disconnected from life support.

There was no autopsy, and not a single photo was taken of the accident scene. It was a textbook example of how not to investigate a death.

Williams drove to Marion, Illinois, for the funeral and burial but skipped the reception afterwards. Driving back to St. Louis, he talked with his son about the many wonders of JoAnn Notheis.

"All the way home he was talking about how we've got to go on," his son, Brett, told the *St. Louis Post-Dispatch*. "He was saying, 'You know, I really like JoAnn a lot.'" When they arrived home, JoAnn Notheis was waiting for him.

Ten weeks later, on December 27, Walter Notheis—home briefly for the holidays between gigs in the Northeast—left his house on Pershing Drive to run an errand, according to his wife. JoAnn said he told her that he was going to an automotive shop to buy a new battery for his Lincoln automobile. He was never seen alive again.

The next day, authorities found his car parked at the St. Louis airport, which they had searched at JoAnn Notheis's suggestion. Continuing the pattern of investigative bumbling that began with the death of Sharon Williams, Walter's car was not impounded. Instead, it was turned over to Jim Williams.

Hours after Walter went missing, Williams moved into his home and his bed. The new lovebirds each had lost a spouse in a matter of weeks. Even Deputy Barney Fife could have sniffed out a love triangle. But the authorities in St. Charles, the most affluent county in Missouri and hardly a hick backwater, with a population approaching 300,000 in a sophisticated major metropolitan area, were essentially clueless. Worse, the lack of a diligent investigation left authorities with little evidence to work with once it finally did occur to the local criminal justice professionals that perhaps a murder or two had been committed.

The turning point was the appointment of Mary Case as St. Charles County chief medical examiner in 1986. Case, a native of Jefferson City, Missouri, was a medical doctor with a professional interest in pathology and head injuries. She had served for six years as an assistant medical examiner in St. Louis when she was hired by

St. Charles. (She would go on to a long career as chief medical examiner for four counties in the St. Louis metro area.)

To his credit, Sheriff Edward Uebinger asked Case to help his office take a fresh look at the death of Sharon Williams and disappearance of Walter Notheis. His investigators had interviewed Jim Williams a week after Walter disappeared, but the session went nowhere. By the time Case was hired, nearly three years had gone by, and Williams and JoAnn were living as newlyweds.

Dr. Case secured legal authorization to exhume Sharon Williams's body from the family cemetery plot in Illinois. The casket was raised on April 1, 1987, and taken to the St. Louis County morgue for a belated autopsy. Case found that the massive injuries to the back of the victim's head were not consistent with those she might have incurred in a car wreck. She saw the accident for what it was: a ham-handed attempt to cover up murder. Case diagnosed homicide, and Big Jim Williams found himself under arrest.

Coincidentally, Williams's oldest son, Jimi, was imprisoned in Florida on a drug rap. Father and son had grown estranged, and Missouri investigators traveled to the Sunshine State to ask Jimi Williams whether he might know anything about the demise of his mother and the disappearance of Walter Notheis Jr. He said he believed his father probably killed both. Asked where dad might have concealed the singer's body, Jimi Williams replied, "What about the cistern?" And that tip is what led authorities to Walter Notheis's body in the tank on Jim Williams's former property on Gutermuth Road in St. Charles. Soon JoAnn Williams joined her new husband as a suspect in the murder of their former spouses.

It was not a simple prosecution. The shoddy investigation gave defense attorneys, led by Michael Turken, a briefcase full of legal ammunition (spelled out in more than one hundred defense motions), and it took another five years to finally get the cases into a courtroom. The murder case against Jim Williams went to trial in the fall of 1992, a full nine years after the two slayings.

Even the passage of so many years did not diminish the puzzlement of many who had been at the scene of the Sharon Williams car wreck. Rescuers Rich Podhorn and Jeffrey Keller testified that the woman reeked of gasoline, even though the gas tank had not been ruptured in the wreck. Lynn Behrens, an intensive care nurse who helped treat the victim, said Sharon was saturated with gasoline from head to toe.

The jury of six men and six women also heard testimony that Williams had stalked Walter Notheis in the days before he disappeared and had asked his employees if they could suggest a hit man. The trial was mercifully swift for the loved ones of the victims, who had waited so long for justice. After barely a week of testimony, the jury took just four hours to convict Williams of both murders.

Prosecutor Thomas Dittmeier argued for the death penalty. "This whole case turns on greed and convenience," he said. "Sharon Williams and Walter Scott stood in Jim Williams's way."

But the jury voted to spare Williams, and Judge E. Richard Webber sentenced him to life without parole. He appealed his conviction relentlessly, to no avail. Big Jim Williams spent his seventieth birthday behind bars in 2009, after nearly two decades locked up at Missouri's Potosi prison, a maximum-security facility south of St. Louis. Unless he wins a mercy release, he'll exit prison in a pine box.

A few weeks after her husband was convicted, JoAnn Williams agreed to plead guilty to hindering the prosecution. Murder charges were dropped, and she served just eighteen months of a five-year sentence. After a decade in the headlines, she slipped into media obscurity following her parole.

In Act II of *Hamlet*, his crime masterpiece, Shakespeare wrote, "For murder, though it have no tongue, will speak with most miraculous organ." It is the most difficult of crimes to get away with, in most cases. Yet Jim Williams and his comely accomplice nearly did—not because they were crime geniuses, but because the investigating authorities were not.

Neither of those involved in the killings has admitted their culpability publicly, so their motives have never been fully revealed. Of course, they succumbed to lust and greed, the terrible twins of the Seven Deadly Sins. But the loved ones of their victims, including six children, were left to ponder the evergreen question for love triangle murders: Why not divorce?

After his death, Walter Notheis gained a measure of the music immortality that escaped him in life. His work on "The Cheater" helped earn Bob Kuban and the In-Men a place in the Rock and Roll Hall of Fame in Cleveland—in a permanent exhibit about one-hit wonders.

CHAPTER 5

Kansas City's
Invisible Serial Killer

The most prolific serial killer in Missouri history has a name that all but the most ardent followers of crime headlines won't recognize. Lorenzo J. Gilyard was a garbage collector in Kansas City who lived his life with a seething rage against women that erupted periodically in sexual violence. After a decade as a pitiless rapist, he turned to the ultimate domination crime: murder.

On a spring night in 1977, Gilyard, then twenty-six years old, began strangling prostitutes in his hometown. By the time he stopped, in 1993, he is believed to have killed at least thirteen women—more than double the number attributed to Jack the Ripper, the prototype prostitute-slayer who did his deadly work in London's East End in the 1880s. But infamy has become increasingly difficult to attain in modern America, with the glut of competition for true-crime headlines.

"It used to be that you'd murder two or three people, and everyone in the country would know your name," Thomas Carroll, a retired crime and sociology professor at the University of Missouri–Kansas City, told me. "Now, a guy kills thirteen, and nobody's ever heard of him."

"Murders are popular infotainment grist, but they need something to move them up the info-news ladder to get media attention, particularly any attention beyond local and regional news," said Ray Surette, a professor of criminology at the University of Central Florida. There is no longer a correlation between the number of victims and public interest, he said.

"A serial killer who murders five people today is competing with all the serial killers paraded across the media over the past generation," Surette said. "Unless there's an additional newsworthy factor—a celebrity connection, a particular gruesomeness, an unusual occupation of the killer, an ideal victim—they are not going to generate the coverage that they might have a generation ago when there was less serial-killer competition."

Gilyard's victims certainly were not celebrities. They lived on the margins of society, and they became further marginalized in death. When they were murdered, few people noticed. That's one of the reasons prostitutes make such easy marks for pathological killers. As Gary Ridgway, the Green River serial killer, once famously said of the forty-eight prostitutes he murdered in the Northwest, "They were just pieces of trash."

Violent psychopaths like Ridgway have long found convenient victims among streetwalkers. These women's clients are not required to produce references, and police feel little pressure to solve the case when they turn up dead. They are throwaway victims. Virtually every sizable American city has been visited by a serial prostitute-killer in the past century, including New Orleans, Phoenix, San Diego, Seattle, Los Angeles, Indianapolis, Detroit, Rochester, Daytona Beach, and Atlantic City. And it's not just an American phenomenon.

Dozens of other countries have experienced the same thing. In one famous example, Andrei Chikatilo murdered fifty-three females, many of them prostitutes, in Rostov, Russia, between 1978 and 1990, earning the nickname the Rostov Ripper.

Kansas City has had more than its share of night-stalkers. Once a provincial cow town known as the home of the secondhand emotions of Hallmark greeting cards, Kansas City today is a sprawling metropolis of two million people. Kansas Citians regard themselves as a mixture of Midwest common sense and Western adventurous spirit. The city might also be properly known as a lodestone for serial killers. Just since the 1980s, Kansas City has hosted at least five serial killers of women, many of the victims sex workers or drug addicts.

Lorenzo Gilyard's competition for designation as Missouri's most prolific murderer is another prostitute-killer from the other side of the state. The sadistic Maury Travis tortured and killed at least twelve hookers in the St. Louis area from 2000 to 2002. He was caught when, in a gambit for attention, he sent a reporter a document downloaded from the Internet that was traced to his computer. He hanged himself in jail after he was arrested.

Successful serial killers of prostitutes—those, like Gilyard, who do their dark work over the course of many years—manage to slip in and out of the shadowy edges of the sex-trade zones in their cities. They compulsively plan their next attack, and the gratification they gain from a fresh murder seems to sustain them for awhile. And when they are not killing, most manage to blend in.

So it was with Lorenzo Gilyard. His life could not have seemed more normal. He and his wife lived in the last house on a dead-end stub of Kenwood Avenue in the black, working-class neighborhood of Waldo in south Kansas City. The homes on his block, all mid-century ranch-styles or split-levels, are tidy but not showy. Gilyard's house bore the usual totems of normality: a Kansas City Chiefs insignia on the garage door, a satellite TV dish in the backyard. The home, shingled and painted forest green, abuts a grassy slope leading up to a shuttered school building. The chain-link fence around his backyard features signs warning, "Beware of Dog" and "Property Under Surveillance."

Clearly, Lorenzo Gilyard wanted to be left alone.

Sexual violence is rooted in control and domination, not libido. Rape is an expression of power and anger and is often committed in retaliation for brutality in the perpetrator's past. In other words, the violent acts of men like Gilyard are the conclusion of a life story, not the beginning. Gilyard has never revealed whether he was subjected to physical brutality as a child, but he certainly had savagery in his genes. His father, Lorenzo Sr., was imprisoned for rape in 1970, and three of his offspring would follow in his footsteps, serving life sentences for violent crimes.

Lorenzo's sister, Patricia Dixon, born in 1958, was a prostitute who stabbed a customer to death in 1983 and was later convicted of second-degree murder in the slaying of another hooker. As of 2010, she was serving life in prison in Missouri. Another of Lorenzo's siblings, Darryl, born in 1953, is serving life without parole in Missouri for a 1989 drug murder. Even before the murder, Darryl Gilyard had his own notoriety in the state. He won a settlement of $4.3 million in 1986 after his legs were severed in a garbage truck accident. Now the millionaire double-amputee murderer pays the state more than $12,000 a year for prison room and board.

But even in a family like that, Lorenzo Gilyard stood out.

He was born May 24, 1950, and grew to a stocky 5-foot-9, with hands like bear claws. As a teenager, he took up the family tradition of pathological violence, bullying and beating women, including the first of his four wives, whom he married at age seventeen when she got pregnant. She would later say in court that Gilyard had subjected her to five years of torture before she escaped. In his teens and early twenties, Gilyard accumulated a long record of rape accusations. It was a different era, when criminal justice protocols put the onus on the victims. Gilyard's accusers, including two acquaintances and a stripper, were reticent to testify against him, and he escaped conviction in each case. His luck changed in 1975, when he was charged with raping the thirteen-year-old daughter of a friend. Gilyard was allowed to plead guilty to mere molestation and was sentenced to just nine months in prison. According to the *Kansas City Star*, a psychiatrist who examined Gilyard as part of a competency test in the child rape case reached the stunning conclusion that he should not be required to undergo psychotherapy or any other form of methodical mental health treatment to address the issues underlying his predatory nature. In this case, Missouri authorities wasted a chance to fix a deeply troubled psyche. Gilyard would prove that shrink dead wrong.

Gilyard's murder spree began in 1977, just months after he was paroled. He developed a distinctive pattern in his homicides from the beginning, favoring very young sex workers—not so different in age from his thirteen-year-old rape victim—that he picked up on the edges of downtown or along prostitution alleys on Troost Avenue, south of the city's skyscrapers. He discarded many of the bodies in a cluster of locations within blocks of one another in southeast Kansas City, not far from the Westport entertainment district—at 38th and Wyandotte, 37th and Garfield, 45th and Euclid, 37th and Troost, and 36th and Broadway. Most of the victims were strangled, a tactile act of domination, after sex. Many were found without shoes, and several had clothing or paper stuffed in their mouths, perhaps to muffle screams. Many of the bodies had been hurriedly dumped—in bushes outside a church in one case, and just steps from the concrete lions at the approach to the majestic Kansas City Life Insurance Building in another. The bodies of several other victims were carefully posed, a postmortem ritual not uncommon among serial killers.

Each of his first three victims, killed over a five-year period, was a wayward teenager working as a novice street prostitute. Stacie Swofford, seventeen, was killed in April 1977 and left to molder amid the trash in an overgrown lot. Gwen Kizine, the youngest victim at fifteen, was left dead in an alley in January 1980. Margaret Miller, seventeen, was found in a vacant lot in May 1982. Kizine's murder rated the most press attention of the three because she was so young. Relatives described her as a happy-go-lucky kid who had attended a fundamentalist church but took a wrong turn toward narcotics, the companion crime of prostitution.

Even amid this killing, Gilyard continued on his well-worn path of brutality, assaulting friends, relatives, and strangers. Two years after murdering his first victim, he was charged in 1979 with raping a woman while holding a gun on her boyfriend. A jury acquitted him, despite compelling evidence. In 1980, he was convicted of assaulting his third wife, who divorced him. He then stalked and beat her twice while the case was under appeal. He murdered Margaret Miller, his third victim, just eight days before he surrendered to serve time for the wife-beating and other charges. Gilyard was imprisoned from May 1982 until January 1986, and the serial killings of Kansas City prostitutes temporarily ceased.

Two months after he was paroled, the slayings resumed with an eight-murder jag over less than two years. On March 14, 1986, the body of Catherine Barry was found in a tumbledown building. Barry, a thirty-four-year-old mother of three, was living on the streets after a mental breakdown. Two more women were killed fourteen weeks apart that year—Naomi Kelly, twenty-three, found on August 16, and Debbie Blevins, thirty-two, found on Thanksgiving Day. Kelly, a single mother, was strangled in a needle park downtown. Blevins, wearing only socks, was dumped outside a church.

Five more bodies turned up in 1987. A stripper named Ann Barnes, the oldest of Gilyard's victims at thirty-six, was found murdered on April 17, 1987, which was both Good Friday and the ten-year anniversary of the murder of Stacie Swofford, Gilyard's first victim. Seven weeks later, Kellie Ann Ford, a twenty-year-old junkie hooker, was found strangled in a park. On September 12, the shoeless corpse of Angela Mayhew, nineteen, was dumped in North Kansas City. Next to go was Sheila Ingold, thirty-six, who was found dead on November 3, in a van on Troost Avenue. Carmeline Hibbs, thirty, was found murdered on December 19 in a Broadway parking lot.

Police knew they had a serial killer on their hands. Many of the women were naked and shoeless, and detectives had a notion that a foot fetishist was at work. The victims ranged from age fifteen to thirty-six. Two-thirds were white, the others black. Many of the women had broken fingernails; they had fought for their lives. Most were garroted with whatever was at hand—their own clothing, an electrical cord, a thick shoestring.

Kansas City was not particularly discomfited by the serial murders. The spree barely registered in the media. Someone ponied up a $1,000 reward—less than a hundred bucks per victim. The pace of the prostitute killings slowed after the surge in 1986 and 1987. The body of Helga Kruger, twenty-six, an Austrian national, was found on Troost Avenue on February 12, 1989. Four years later, in January 1993, Connie Luther was found dead. That murder, Gilyard's last, rated about one hundred words deep inside the local news section of the *Kansas City Star*:

> The nude body of a Kansas City woman was found Monday on a sidewalk on the city's West Side. The woman, Connie Luther, 29, was found about 6:30 A.M. near 25th and Allen streets, investigators said. Police think she was killed elsewhere. A man who was driving to work Monday told police he discovered Luther's nude body face down in the snow among leaves and trash. Police have no suspects or motive. An autopsy will be performed to determine the cause of death.

The most important crime stories often spring not from the unusual cases, but from the routine ones. Good crime reporters, like good cops, manage to connect the dots that give significance to seemingly insignificant events. In this case, there was a story buried in those hundred words about Connie Luther's demise—the story of Lorenzo Gilyard's secret life as a killer.

There is an adage in law enforcement that pathological serial killers only stop when they are caught or they die. But Gilyard defied conventional wisdom: He stopped. He had taken a job as a garbage collector after his release from prison in 1986. His boss at Deffenbaugh Disposal Service said Gilyard was punctual, personable, and reliable. Gilyard was promoted to a supervisory job.

He lived with his fourth wife, Jackie, whom he married in 1991, in the house in the Waldo section of town. They were not particularly friendly to their neighbors. Gilyard was nettled by turnarounds in his driveway—not infrequent since theirs was the last house on a dead-end street—so he posted his property with a "Do Not Enter" sign. One neighbor lady moved away because she believed Gilyard was a Peeping Tom.

On October 30, 1989, Gilyard took another female neighbor to dinner. She demurred when Gilyard suggested sex, and he reacted true to form: with violence. The woman said Gilyard held a knife to his own throat and threatened suicide unless she complied with his sexual demands. She did so but went to police. Under a plea deal, Gilyard was required to undergo sex and anger counseling. But the therapy was too late to save the many victims of his sex assaults and murders—nearly two dozen in all.

As the years passed, the serial murders of lowly prostitutes moved lower and lower in priority as detectives focused on fresh cases. Gilyard must have believed that he got away with it. And he might have, had it not been for a federal grant. Since the 1990s, advances in DNA technology have pushed scores of the world's police departments to form cold-case squads. Kansas City joined them, publicizing the squad with an unfortunate photo showing its seven members posed in a cooler amid blocks of ice, wearing "Untouchable"–era fedoras.

Old-school detective work may solve some cases, but a more appropriate cold-case PR photo would show a crime lab tech using the "rif-lip" technique ("restriction fragment length polymorphism") to compare DNA molecules. That is how the Gilyard case was solved—after languishing in detective bureau purgatory for decades. In 2003, Kansas City police received a $111,000 federal grant to apply DNA-testing technology to evidence in cold cases. The money was used primarily to pay technicians to work overtime, focusing on a backlog of some six hundred unsolved murders and rapes with stored evidence. Detectives helped select eighty-five cases that showed promise of being solved. One of them was the murder of Naomi Kelly, the second of Gilyard's three victims in 1986.

The technicians found that DNA from Kelly's killer was a match with genetic evidence stored from eleven other hooker slayings. They didn't have to look far to find a name to attach to the DNA. In 1987, Lorenzo Gilyard had agreed to give a blood sample as part of the serial-killer investigation. He was known to patronize prostitutes, and hookers told cops they were frightened of him. The blood did not solve the case, but his sample had been kept on file for seventeen years.

On April 16, 2004, Gilyard, fifty-three, was arrested as he was eating dinner at a Denny's restaurant. He was charged with twelve counts of first-degree murder. Sergeant John Jackson of the Kansas City police cold-case squad was filled with self-congratulation about breaking the case, calling it a "trophy day." But the fact is that science solved the murders, not detective work. The most prolific killer in Missouri history had been hiding under the police department's nose since 1987, and he might never have been identified without the lab's forensic work. Loved ones of the victims cheered police, but the criminal justice system had failed the women by attaching such low priority to their murders.

Although Gilyard claimed innocence by rote, he plotted a defense strategy to avoid execution. Jackson County, Missouri, prosecutor Jim Kanatzar said he would not seek the death penalty if Gilyard agreed to a trial without a jury and a waiver of most of his rights to appeal a guilty verdict. Kanatzar said the agreement ensured a "quick, just and final disposition." Even after Judge John O'Malley threw out much of the evidence collected against Gilyard in 1987 and after his arrest in 2004, citing sloppy police work, Kanatzar still had uncontestable DNA evidence to work with. He prosecuted Gilyard for seven murders committed during the spree of 1986 and 1987—the slayings of Ann Barnes, Catherine Barry, Kellie Ford, Carmeline Hibbs, Sheila Ingold, Naomi Kelly, and

Angela Mayhew. DNA from semen evidence linked Gilyard to six of the seven, and a hair provided the evidence in the murder of Mayhew. It was a businesslike trial, often the case when there is no jury. Judge O'Malley convicted Gilyard of six counts of murder after a trial that lasted barely a week. He was acquitted in the Mayhew murder.

On April 13, 2007, Gilyard—slimmed down by forty pounds after three years in custody—stood before O'Malley to hear his sentence of life without parole. Gilyard spoke just eight nihilistic words: "No matter what I say, it doesn't matter."

O'Malley delivered a stern lecture, saying Gilyard had "forfeited any right to live out here among the rest of us." He called his actions "obscene insults to our sense of justice, security and freedom." The judge said he hoped that Gilyard would spend his lifetime in prison reflecting on what he had done to get there.

But the judge's idealized concept of personal remorse would require a conscience, something Lorenzo Gilyard never displayed in a lifetime of violence against women. And it would require him to admit guilt—something else he had never done. Perhaps that is because for Gilyard to confess to multiple murders committed over seventeen years would be tantamount to him admitting that he is a monster.

CHAPTER 6

"A Total Waste":
Murder on a Bridge

Every murder, every crime, is an abomination to someone. But certain transgressions stand out for their callousness, their lack of compassion, or their fundamental recklessness. In the vast archive of heartless human acts, one particular example from the State of Missouri deserves a position in the pantheon of senselessness. A college professor who taught writing to the two victims, Julie and Robin Kerry, had a perfect, succinct summary of the crime: "It was such a total waste."

It all began with the old Chain of Rocks Bridge over the Mississippi River upstream from St. Louis. The mile-long bridge was built in 1929 in the Warren truss style, the classic crisscrossed web of iron, about nine miles north of downtown St. Louis. It was the first bridge you come to downstream from the confluence of the Mississippi and Missouri rivers. The Chain of Rocks got its name from a dangerous shoal of boulders there, once the sole impediment in the Mighty Mississippi's nine-foot-deep channel from St. Paul, Minnesota, to its milk chocolate–colored ooze into the Gulf of Mexico, 1,200 miles away.

The bridge, with a distinctive, 22-degree bend near its center, links the very northern tip of the City of St. Louis with Chouteau Island in Granite City, Illinois. It rests just north of the vast St. Louis Waterworks plant, and two elaborately designed water intakes stand just downstream from it, like miniature castles. The bridge was an official part of the famous Route 66 in the 1950s, when transportation authorities—dealing with traffic issues even then—rerouted the old federal highway onto a bypass that stayed north of congested downtown St. Louis. For decades, Gateway City denizens spent summer days in the shadow of the bridge at the Chain of Rocks Amusement Park, which was shuttered in the mid-1970s. President Eisenhower's interstate highway system made the old bridge obsolete. The feds built a new Mississippi crossing for Interstate 270, just upstream, and the old bridge was barricaded in 1968. The government discussed tearing it down, but the cost was prohibitive. Instead, officials barred it with fencing and dumped a rock pile on the Missouri side to dissuade entry. But for generations, kids have managed to find their way onto abandoned bridges.

During the 1970s and 1980s, the old Chain of Rocks became a party spot for teenagers, who clambered over the rock pile and through the fence. Some would simply walk to Illinois and back. Others would lug along a twelve-pack, and empty beer cans would tumble seventy-five feet to the water below. Cops from St. Louis and Granite City were frequent visitors, shooing away miscreants and youngsters or investigating petty crimes reported to have occurred there.

Like all old bridges, the Chain of Rocks had its share of graffiti. Much of it was the familiar obscenities and urban name-tagging. In the summer of 1989, an unusual variety of graffiti turned up, stretching more than fifty feet near the state line marker at the middle of the bridge. It was a plea for racial harmony—borrowing the title of the contemporary Spike Lee film, *Do the Right Thing*:

> United we stand/Divided we fall
> It's not a black or white thing
> We as a new generation
> Have got to take a stand
> Unite as one. We've Got 2 stop killing one another
> You don't have to be black or white to feel prejudice
> To fall in love, experience pain, create life
> To kill, to die. You just have to be human.
> Do the right thing.

The authors of the message were Julie and Robin Kerry, sisters from the St. Louis suburb of Spanish Lake, three miles from the bridge. They were daughters of Virginia Kerry, a legal secretary, and Richard Kerry, a dentist. There were two other Kerry sisters—Kathleen, the oldest, and Jamie, the youngest. Their parents had separated in 1987, and the daughters lived with their mother.

Julie and Robin, a year apart in age and each 5-foot-1 and barely 100 pounds, were sensitive children. Julie affixed a dictum to the wall of her basement bedroom: "Who says you can't change the world?" Her mother told the *St. Louis Post-Dispatch* that her children lived that philosophy. The peace sign was their personal totem. The girls were raised with a broad worldview, even though they did not stray far from home for their education: they attended St. Jerome Catholic Grade School in Bissell Hills, just across I-270 from their home; Hazelwood East High School, within walking distance of home; and the University of Missouri at St. Louis, five miles from Spanish Lake.

In the spring of 1991, Julie was twenty years old and Robin nineteen. Each was highly regarded at their university, where Julie was a sophomore English major and Robin a freshman studying languages. Julie hoped for a career as a writer, and her little sister seemed destined for a life of social activism. They advocated on behalf of the homeless and the environment. They were generous with their time and money, sometimes opting to give to charity the cash they would have otherwise spent on gifts for their parents and siblings. The sisters were proud of the ode they painted on the old Chain of Rocks Bridge. And it was that message that took them there on a warm spring night in 1991.

The Kerrys's cousin, Tom Cummins, age nineteen, had arrived in St. Louis on March 29 to visit his grandparents. Cummins was scheduled to leave the morning of April 5 to return home to Wheaton, Maryland, where he had just begun work as a fire department paramedic. Julie Kerry wanted to take Cummins to the bridge to show her cousin their graffiti. Their last chance was late at night on April 4, and the two sisters and Cummins rendezvoused for a midnight trip to Chain of Rocks in Julie's Chevette. They parked, and then made their way over and around the various barriers to the bridge deck.

They were not alone. As the Kerrys and their cousin walked toward the Illinois side, they saw four young men approaching from the opposite direction. The four seemed to be led by the largest among them, Marlin Gray, twenty-three, who was 6-foot-4 and weighed more than 200 pounds. He introduced himself to the cousins as "Marlin from Wentzville." An unemployed aspiring songwriter, he lived in Wentzville, an exurban city of 25,000 at the far western edge of St. Charles County, 45 miles from downtown St. Louis. Also in the group was short and stocky Antonio Richardson, sixteen, a troubled kid who lived in Pine Lawn, an impoverished town just outside the St. Louis city limits where hundreds of poor black families moved when the ghetto neighborhoods of Chestnut Valley and Mill Creek Valley were razed in the 1950s. The third man was Richardson's cousin, Reginald Clemons, nineteen, a gangly shade-tree mechanic who lived around the corner from Richardson in Pine Lawn. Last was Daniel Winfrey, a wispy fifteen-year-old who, like Gray, lived in Wentzville, where he was a high school freshman. Winfrey had met Gray just a few weeks before.

The Kerry sisters, Cummins, and Winfrey were white. Gray, Clemons, and Richardson were black. The four men had arrived on the bridge about thirty minutes before the Kerry group. They later said they had journeyed there on a whim after drinking beer and smoking a joint. They insisted that they had gone to the bridge with no particular idea in mind.

Winfrey bummed a cigarette from the sisters, and the two groups chatted amicably. Marlin Gray showed the cousins how to climb down a manhole from the bridge deck to gain access to the concrete bridge support below. Gray told Cummins it was a suitable place to be "alone with your woman."

The two groups parted ways after a few minutes. The sisters showed their cousin the poem, then continued toward Illinois, stopping to gaze at a campfire down below along the wooded riverbank.

As the other group walked back toward Missouri, Clemons said he had an idea: Why not rob the cousins? Marlin Gray is said to have clapped his hands over the idea. "Yeah, I feel like hurting somebody," he said. The four turned and walked back toward Illinois. Gray dug condoms out of his pocket and handed one to each of his companions. When Winfrey waved him off, Gray pinned him to the bridge railing and said, "You're gonna do it."

When the four reached the cousins, they turned and followed closely behind them. Near midspan, at the bend in the bridge just beyond the Kerrys's poem, Marlin Gray sidled up to Cummins. He put an arm around his shoulder, walked him back about fifteen feet and said, "This isn't your lucky night. This is a robbery. Get down on the ground." He added, "I've never had the privilege of popping somebody. If you put your head up or try to look, I'm going to pop you."

The four then accosted Julie and Robin Kerry, who screamed and fought against the attackers. The assailants threatened to throw them off the bridge unless they piped down. Someone among the four asked, "Do you want to die?"

The young women were forced to the deck, stripped, and raped, with the men taking turns—one pinning a victim's arms while another committed rape, then switching places. When the barbaric assaults were finished, Cummins was robbed of his wallet, watch, cash, and keys. The assailants were spooked to find his fire department badge in the wallet, which they mistook for a police shield. Cummins said he overhead two of the men discuss whether to kill him. One of the men told him, "We know who you are, and if you tell anybody, we're going to come and get you."

The assailants forced the naked sisters and their cousin down the manhole onto a metal platform below the bridge deck. A judge later summarized what happened next:

"Clemons ordered Cummins and the Kerry sisters to step out onto the concrete pier below the metal platform. The three were told not to touch each other. Julie Kerry and then Robin were pushed from the pier of the bridge, falling a distance of 50 to 70 feet to the water. Cummins was then told to jump. Believing his chances of survival were better if he jumped instead of being pushed, he jumped from the bridge."

Clemons and Richardson ran to catch up with Winfrey and Gray, who had walked further toward the Missouri side after the rapes. Clemons told them, "We threw them off! Let's go!" The four sprinted to their car—a Chevy Citation owned by Gray's girlfriend—and sped off. They drove north up Lewis and Clark Boulevard through Spanish Lake, passing just blocks from the home of the Kerry sisters, then across the Highway 67 Bridge to Alton, Illinois. They stopped at a gas station and bought snacks with the cash taken from Cummins. They then drove on to a Mississippi River overlook, where they stood and looked down on the scene of their crimes, like an arsonist watching his own fire.

Did they wonder about the irrationality, even insanity, of what had just happened—how an unplanned strong-arm robbery, a simple crime of opportunity, had morphed into gang rape and murder? Probably not. They were not that thoughtful. Instead, they high-fived one another. Marlin Gray gave props to sixteen-year-old Richardson for being "brave" in pushing the Kerry sisters off the bridge. Reggie Clemons assured his mates, "They'll never make it to shore."

He was only two-thirds right.

The Kerry sisters and Cummins descended into a Mississippi River swollen from the spring snowmelt. The water was seventeen feet deep where they fell, with a swirling current that was a vestige of the shoal of rocks now far below the surface. Tom Cummins must have been surprised that he surfaced at all after plunging into the roiling water. Then came a second surprise: He heard Julie Kerry cry out. They moved to one another, grasping and clutching. But the flailing woman was pulling them both under, and Cummins and his cousin separated. Soon she was gone forever.

Cummins swam for the Missouri shore and dragged himself out of the water at the city waterworks plant. He ran to nearby Riverview Boulevard and flagged down a passing truck. He spat out his story, and police cars and rescue boats raced to the scene. Robin and Julie Kerry's poor parents got a dreadful middle-of-the-night wakeup.

Police did not believe Tom Cummins was telling the truth. The story seemed so unlikely, the event so cruel. He and his cousins, on a midnight stroll, happened upon a group of four men who raped the young women then pitched them all off a Mississippi River bridge? What sort of beasts could commit such an act? And if it happened the way Cummins said, how did he survive to tell about it?

There was a backstory to the police skepticism. The case of Charles and Carol Stuart was still on the mind of every big-city cop in America. In October 1989, Charles Stuart had shot and killed his pregnant wife in Boston, then concocted a black bogeyman as the murderer. Boston cops blindly bought the story, and the police department was subjected to legitimate criticism about institutional racism when it came to light that the husband was the killer. St. Louis detectives got stuck on the idea that Cummins, too, was lying to cover up his own crimes. He was interrogated at intervals over fifteen hours that day. At some point, the frustrated and exhausted Cummins told the cops, "If you say I did it, then I did it." He was booked as a murder suspect. The front page of the April 6 edition of the *Post-Dispatch* carried the headline, "Two Sisters Missing In N.

County; Police Hold Cousin After Story Of Attack." The story said cops believed the girls had fallen from the bridge while Cummins was making sexual advances.

Who knows how far the pursuit of Cummins as a suspect might have gone? Perhaps forensic evidence—semen, fingerprints—would have turned up on the bridge deck to back up his story. It's likely that the four killers, two of them not yet old enough to legally drive a car, would have been revealed by the amateur criminal's customary method of detection: his own blabbing mouth. This crime story was destined to become front-page news nationwide, and surely one of the four would have given in to the temptation to take credit among his peers.

But a single piece of forgotten evidence immediately turned the focus of the probe away from Tom Cummins. In their rush to leave the crime scene, the killers had left an oversized flashlight on the bridge, where police found it. The owner had gone through the trouble of marking it "Horn 1." The *Post-Dispatch* carried a photo of a cop holding the flashlight in its April 6 story. Police suggested the owner of the flashlight might have been a witness.

The legitimate owner wasn't a witness, but his information solved the crimes. Ron Whitehorn, a bus driver and former deputy sheriff, called police to claim the flashlight. It had been stolen, he said, by a neighbor kid who was visiting his daughter one day. He gave police the name of the thief: Antonio Richardson, the sixteen-year-old among the Chain of Rocks four.

Richardson gave up his fellow felons, and all four were soon arrested and indicted for murder, rape, and robbery. They had spread the evidence around between them. Gray had Tom Cummins's watch. Clemons had his fire department badge. Richardson left his fingerprints on Cummins's Maryland driver's license. Following standard form for group crimes, those three blamed each other and gave accounts that minimized their own participation. But from the beginning, prosecutor Nels Moss Jr. focused on a crime narrative in which Marlin Gray, the oldest and largest, was the ringleader. Moss had a golden case once Winfrey, the youngest suspect, agreed to plead guilty to second-degree murder and testify against his companions. Gray's trial came first, in the fall of 1992, and jurors listened to a recording of his forty-eight-minute confession, in which he acknowledged rape and robbery but denied pushing the sisters to their deaths. Cummins testified about the horror of listening to his cousins scream as they descended to the water.

Prosecutor Moss gave a withering account of the lack of mercy that night:

> They led them to the hole and they slaughtered them without benefit of court, without benefit of attorney, without benefit of a judge, without benefit of somebody being able to speak in their behalf. These fellows executed these people as surely as they have put a bullet in their head. The decision to walk them to the hole. The decision to lay them on the platform. The decision to get them up off the platform. The decision to put them on the pier. The decision to push one off. The decision to push the second one off. The decision to tell Thomas Cummins that he better jump or he's gonna get shot . . . We're talking cool reflection, these are the decisions that these people have had the opportunity to make over a period of time of many minutes . . . It wasn't in sudden passion. It wasn't in anger. This was cool and calculating.

Gray was convicted of first-degree murder, and Judge Thomas Mummert sentenced him to die. Reggie Clemons and Antonio Richardson, who pushed the sisters to their deaths, according to Winfrey, met the same fates at trials held in 1993—conviction and condemnation. After nearly a decade on Death Row, Richardson's sentence was commuted to life in prison in 2003 after appeals based in part upon the fact that he was sixteen at the time of the offenses.

Marlin Gray fought long and hard against his own death sentence, claiming that he was less culpable because he did not push the sisters; that his conviction was beaten out of him, and that he was a victim of racism. His appeals failed, and his comeuppance arrived nearly fifteen years after the murders. His final statement was another denial of guilt: "I go forward now on wings built by the love and support of my family and friends. I go with a peace of mind that comes from never having taken a human life. I forgive those who have hardened their hearts to the truth and I pray they ask forgiveness, for they know not what they do. This is not a death, it is a lynching." A few minutes after midnight on October 26, 2005, the State of Missouri ended Gray's life by lethal injection.

Daniel Winfrey, sentenced to thirty years in prison, served half of that. He won early parole in 2007, at the prosecutor's encouragement, for having played a role in winning convictions against the other three. The fourth, Clemons, is still on Death Row at Potosi Correctional Center in Mineral Point, Missouri. As of 2010, he had spent half his life waiting to die.

Julie Kerry's body was found three hundred miles downstream from Chain of Rocks three weeks after that horrible night on the bridge. Her sister's remains were never found. Tom Cummins sued St. Louis authorities over the heavy-handed police interrogation and their statements to the media that implicated him in his cousins' murders. He eventually settled for $150,000. Cummins's sister wrote a book about the murders and the everlasting aftermath. The Kerrys's youngest sibling, Jamie, became a poet, like her departed sisters.

Years ago, Virginia Kerry told a reporter that she had a simple wish.

"I don't want the world to forget Julie and Robin Kerry," she said. "I don't want the world to forget what they believed in and what they fought for."

In 1999, the fencing and rock pile were removed, and the old Chain of Rocks Bridge reopened as part of a public hiking trail along the St. Louis riverfront. Walkers can make their way to the spot where the girls were pushed toward the dirty water below, a short stroll from their faded "Do the Right Thing" message.

Over the years, some commentators have used the oblique irony of the murders to buttress racist inclinations: white sisters raped and slain by thee black men and a white hanger-on just steps away from their ode to racial harmony. One fool called it a case of "poetic justice."

The Kerry sisters would have been horrified. There was no justice in their murders. It was a total waste—nothing more, nothing less.

CHAPTER 7

Missouri Pastoral:
Disorder on the Farm

Chillicothe, an orderly farm community in northern Missouri, does not seem to be the sort of place that would harbor a pathological criminal. The city of nine thousand is one of those red, white, and blue towns, authentically all-American. Located an hour east of St. Joseph on the Grand River, Chillicothe markets itself as "The City in the Country." It is the seat of government for Livingston County, where it sits smack-dab in the middle, at the intersection of U.S. Highways 65 and 36.

A few years ago, Chillicothe discovered that it was the home of an unusual American "first." In 1928, the Chillicothe Baking Company became the first firm in the United States to use a new invention: the bread-slicing machine. When news of this event, obscured for seventy-five years, was unearthed for a local history book, the city began a new marketing campaign: "Chillicothe: Home of Sliced Bread."

Chillicothe needed an image makeover, after what Ray and Faye Copeland had done to its reputation. The Copelands lived ten miles to the west of the city, on a small farm outside the hamlet of Mooresville. But when the story of their lives as Missouri's most curious modern killers made the national news, the dateline was Chillicothe—always Chillicothe.

As much as anything, Ray Copeland was a testament to the inadequacies of a fourth-grade education. He was a lousy thief, despite a lifetime of practice. He failed as a farmer but was too mulish to give up. He finally earned infamy in his dotage by trying one last plot: an absurd murder-for-profit scheme that brought together all of his carefully hewed deficiencies. Early in life, the nearly illiterate Copeland grew captivated by the idea that he could scrawl his signature on a worthless check and trade it for a valuable commodity— cattle on the hoof, for example. He fiddled with forgery schemes for decades until he struck upon a crazy plan to use disposable stand-ins who would write the worthless checks, then turn the commodity over to him. With the helpers' work complete and their value depleted, Copeland then killed and buried the stand-ins. As a final measure of his incompetence as a farmer, a forger, and a killer, Copeland got caught because he didn't plant his human crop deep enough.

City-dwellers in America tend to view their rural neighbors as industrious and square—law-abiders who live a more wholesome existence than those of us who reside in urban Sodom and Gomorrahs. It is true that Ray Copeland wore bib overalls and occasionally employed a pitchfork, just like the fellow in Grant Wood's *American Gothic*. But Copeland also was living proof that farmers lie, cheat, and steal, just like the rest of us.

He was born in Oklahoma in 1914 and raised in the Arkansas Ozarks near Harrison. (The city, twenty miles south of the Missouri state line, bears a degree of infamy. In the early 1900s, white residents twice ran the entire black population out of town, and it remains predominantly white today.) Copeland's parents, Jess and Laney, were tenant farmers struggling to raise five kids. Ray, who dropped out of school in fourth grade, wasn't much help. Lazy and shiftless, at age twenty he stole two hogs from his father and sold them, commencing a lifelong pattern of filching livestock. Two years later, he was run in for forgery, his other favorite crime. He got a year in jail in Harrison for writing a worthless check.

In 1940, after his parole, Copeland began a romance with Faye Della Wilson, who at nineteen was seven years younger than he was. Faye was raised in a hillbilly shack in Red Star, a dusty spot in the road in the Ozark National Forest of north Arkansas. One of seven children, she quit school after eighth grade, but that still gave her twice as much education as her suitor. Copeland married Faye six months after they met, and Faye bore five children over nine years: Everett in 1941, Billy Ray in 1943, Betty Lou in 1945, Alvia in 1947, and William in 1949.

The newlyweds lived an untethered life, moving frequently to stay a step ahead of the law. Faye later explained that her husband had a lifelong pattern of "messing up," as she called his criminal indiscretions. She said, "I begged him time and time again to please stay out of trouble." He didn't listen. In 1944, with two toddlers in tow and a third child on the way, the Copelands joined the migration west, settling in Fresno, California, a Central Valley farming mecca on the verge of a population and economic boom. The Copelands were positioned to capitalize, but Ray messed up again. He was accused of rustling horses from a neighbor, and he was run out of town in 1951. The family returned to the Midwest, living in Rocky Comfort, in the Ozarks of southern Missouri, and on farms in Illinois. But they were forced to move on as Copeland failed at one criminal connivance after another. He was arrested at least three times for forgery from the mid-1950s to the mid-60s. He was both a lousy crook and a slow learner. In 1961, for example, he spent a year in jail for buying twenty cows with a bad check. A month after he was released, he pulled the same stunt—and was sent back to prison.

In 1966, after yet another parole, the Copelands landed in Chillicothe. The small city suited them, and they settled in, paying $6,000 for a rickety house and 40-acre farm outside nearby Mooresville. Crop and livestock income from 40 acres won't pay a mortgage, so Copeland leased additional farmland in the area. But profits were elusive. Copeland, bald and hard of hearing, earned an odious reputation among his neighbors, who viewed him as gruff and profane. He liked to gripe about bankers and farm equipment suppliers, blaming them for his failures. And he never had a kind word for his wife or children.

Faye, who had supported her brood with factory work during her husband's frequent incarcerations, was forced by her husband to take a job at the Midwest Glove Company in Chillicothe. Ray Copeland could have joined his wife there. He took jobs sporadically off the farm as a handyman or housepainter. But was never able to shake his inclination toward expeditious but illegal routes to quick cash over the commonsense solution to a lack of money: work more often. So while his wife worked, Ray Copeland began to scheme again.

In the late 1970s, when most men his age would have been mulling retirement, Copeland began to plan a new twist on his favorite companion crimes of cattle theft and forgery. What if he could cast himself as a victim of forgery? He needed a crime partner with very different handwriting to sign a check in Copeland's name to buy cattle. The men would quickly resell the livestock and split the profits. The crime partner would disappear, and Copeland, the perpetrator, would claim to be a victim.

Where would he find such a crime partner? Copeland had a spent a lifetime on the move—both as a child, while his father tried unsuccessfully to make a stake as a farmer in one place then another, and as an adult, as his "mess-ups" chased him from one town to the next. He knew from personal experience that itinerants manage to move like ghosts in and out of small cities. And from that idea he made a plan: He would find his partners at soup kitchens and homeless shelters two hundred miles south in Springfield, Missouri.

Against all odds, the scheme apparently worked several times. Copeland and his drifter-partner would sit opposite one another at a cattle auction, and he would prompt his foil when to bid. The partner would sign one of Copeland's checks for a cattle purchase in the $1,500 range. The men would quickly resell the cattle, and Copeland would play dumb when confronted by authorities. Although the signature on the check was not Copeland's, law enforcers knew enough about his criminal history to suspect dishonesty. But the partners had moved on, so investigators couldn't make a case against Copeland.

His luck ran out when he recruited a drifter named Gerald Perkins who stayed around too long. Authorities tracked down Perkins, who provided a thorough account of Ray Copeland's culpability as the mastermind of the false-forgery scam. In his mid-60s, Copeland was yet again sent up the river, serving two years for forgery.

So in his idle time behind bars, he came up with a diabolical modification to the scheme. In the summer of 1989, a farm worker named Jack McCormick stumbled upon a human skull and other bones in a shallow depression in the dirt near a barn on Copeland's farm. He breathlessly reported his discovery to Faye Copeland, whose odd response was to sternly caution McCormick to stay the hell away from that part of the property. Spooked, McCormick tried to file a report with the Livingston County sheriff. When he got short-shrifted there, he made a prudent decision to skedaddle, making his way west to Nebraska. But McCormick could not forget what he had seen. On August 20, 1989, he called a crime tips hotline in Nebraska and reported what he had seen on the Copeland farm. McCormick, fifty-seven, later described himself as a "common gutter tramp and drunk," but he will go down in true-crime history for bringing to light one of the most puzzling murder-for-profit ploys imaginable.

On October 8, 1989, seven weeks after McCormick's tip, forty law enforcers arrived at the Copeland farm with a search warrant and a backhoe. After failing to find human bones there, they shifted their focus the following week to a barn twelve miles away, in Ludlow, Missouri, that Copeland had leased for hay storage. After removing some two thousand bales of hay stacked to the ceiling, investigators found freshly turned dirt on the barn floor. Just below the surface, they unearthed a body wrapped in black plastic—then another, and a third. Each had been killed with a single gunshot to the back of the head. The victims were eventually identified as Paul Cowart, twenty-one, a drifter from Arkansas; John Freeman, twenty-seven, originally from Tulsa; and Jimmie Dale Harvey, twenty-seven, from Springfield, Missouri. A few days later, the body of another transient, Wayne Warner, was found buried in another barn that Copeland had used. A fifth victim, Dennis Murphy, from Normal, Illinois, was found in a twenty-eight-foot-deep well not far from Warner's body.

Murder was the modification of Copeland's forgery scheme. He recruited drifters at shelters, just as in the earlier version, promising $50 a day plus room and board. He would send his new men to small-town banks to open checking accounts, making sizable cash deposits (with Copeland's money) and using a post office box as an address. Copeland would then order the men to withdraw most of the money and return it to him. He would send them to livestock sales, where they would buy cattle with their own rubber checks. Just as before, they would sell the livestock to slaughterhouses or feed lots for pure profit. But instead of sending the men away when their value was depleted, Copeland buried the evidence after putting a .22-caliber slug in the backs of their heads with his Marlin varmint gun.

The murders began in 1986 with Warner and Murphy. Cowart was killed in May 1989, Freeman in December 1988, and Harvey in October 1988. The dates of those deaths led authorities to believe that there must have been other victims—perhaps in the gap year of 1987. Investigators determined that the Copelands pocketed a total of $32,000 from the scheme in 1986, 1988, and 1989. Is it reasonable to believe that the money-hungry Ray Copeland would have taken an unexplained pause in 1987?

When the national news media got hold of the story, the Copelands were first portrayed as struggling farmers who turned to murder out of desperation. The *New York Times* called it a case of "rural intrigue." When the murders came to light, Ray was seventy-five and Faye sixty-eight—with seventeen grandchildren and twenty-five great-grandchildren. And in that era when Farm Aid had become a populist charitable movement, the media dutifully noted that the Copelands were at risk of bankruptcy, buried in $25,000 in farm debt.

Faye Copeland was assumed to have been a reluctant accomplice to a bullying husband. "I never done nothin'," she grumbled during a perp walk.

"I'll always love him, but not as much now," Faye later said of Ray in a jailhouse interview with the *St. Joseph News-Press/Gazette.* "I begged him time and time again to please stay out of trouble. We had our home and everything paid for. We were on Social Security. So why would he turn around and mess all that up just like he has?"

But it turned out that she was implicated by several bits of creepy evidence. Inside the Copeland home, lawmen found hidden in a camera case a ledger containing about two dozen names, all men who had worked as Copeland hired hands. Some of the names had the notation "back" beside them. And twelve names were marked with an ominous X, including all five whose bodies were found and the three others suspected to have been killed but whose bodies were never found. (Four others with an X were later found alive.) The writing was in Faye Copeland's hand.

Authorities also found in the Copeland home a ghoulish keepsake: a quilt, stitched by Faye, made from the clothing of the murdered men. She attracted further suspicion when she passed her husband a jailhouse note urging him to "remain cool." And investigators noted that at least one of the victims had been shot in a room adjacent to Faye Copeland's bedroom.

Both Copelands were charged with five counts of murder, and prosecutors sought the strictest justice, despite their ages. "It's the death penalty because of the nature of the alleged offenses here," said Missouri Attorney General William Webster. "We don't seek to deviate merely because of the age."

Husband and wife faced trial separately. As Faye Copeland's trial date approached, authorities offered a plea bargain: Lead them to the other three graves and walk free. She swore through tears she did not know where the bodies were buried. Ray Copeland tried to offer that information in exchange for freedom for his wife and a guarantee against execution, but the judge declined to accept the plea agreement.

At Faye Copeland's trial in November 1990, her attorneys tried to portray her as a victim of spousal abuse who lived in terror of beatings and bullying. A witness testified that Ray treated her "like trash," and a psychiatrist said the woman had been controlled by her husband for decades. But the trial judge would not allow testimony regarding battered spouse syndrome, nor would he let the defendant's children and neighbors give jurors much detail about the abuse she endured. Faye was convicted of five counts of first-degree murder and sentenced to death by lethal injection, becoming the oldest woman on Death Row in America. She sobbed uncontrollably upon hearing her sentence.

Ray Copeland was not so moved by the news. When the sheriff told him that Faye had been convicted and condemned, he coolly replied, "Well, those things happen to some, you know?"

Shortly after his wife's conviction, Ray Copeland telephoned a *St. Louis Post-Dispatch* reporter from the state psychiatric center where he was being evaluated. He invited the news scribbler to interview him, and those conversations provide the only real glimpse into Copeland's psyche. Of course, he lied through his teeth and tears.

"I never killed anybody in my life," Copeland told Bill Smith of the *Post-Dispatch*. "Me and my wife lived together for fifty years. We never killed nobody. We never hurt nobody, and we never talked about hurting nobody. I hope that me and my wife will fall over dead in the next five minutes if we done this."

Copeland said, "They haven't got no witnesses at all that saw me shoot anybody or bury anybody. Some of these boys stayed with me a week or ten days and then they took their money out of the bank and left. Just because these boys left some dirty clothes and a suitcase at my house and just because they found a list of their names in my house, they think we did it."

But by the date of his trial in March 1991, Ray Copeland had changed tactics. He sought to blame his crazy homicide habit on insanity—or what his lawyer, Barbara Schenkenberg, called "progressive, organic brain damage." The prosecutor had another take on the serial murders. "The grim reality of this case is that we have a hired killer in our midst," said Kenny Hulshof, an assistant state attorney general. "He might wear a pair of work books and bib overalls, but he has a wallet where his heart should be, and he's a killer for cash."

The jury found Copeland guilty, and Judge E. Richard Webber condemned him to die, just like his wife. But by the time his trial ended, Copeland's health was in decline, and he saved taxpayers the expense of execution when he died of natural causes in 1993, at age seventy-eight, at the Potosi state prison.

After her husband's death, Faye Copeland became a cause célèbre. She was portrayed on TV and in newspapers as a battered woman, a know-nothing hick raised in an Arkansas log cabin, a Missouri county fair pickled-beet champion, a harmless great-grandmother, and a model prisoner (known by fellow jailbirds as "Mrs. Faye") with a magic touch at growing flowers.

"I couldn't have flowers at home," she told a *Kansas City Star* scribe in 1999. "He didn't like me to be tending to anything other than him. As long as I was with him or working the cattle or the tractor that was OK. But flowers, no, he didn't like them."

She went on, "I was raised to love my husband and support him no matter what. The man is the head of the family. The Bible says it should be that way. . . Maybe we'd have got along better if I had knocked the shit out of him a few times."

Attorneys filed a stream of appeals on her behalf, arguing that barred testimony about spousal battery and inflammatory arguments by prosecutors had denied the woman a fair trial. In 1999, a federal appeals court overturned her death sentence, ruling the Ray Copeland "not only was the scheme's primary actor, but was also its creator." The judges said there "was substantial evidence that Ray dominated and controlled his wife."

As another judge reconsidered her fate at a 2001 sentencing hearing, Faye Copeland told him, "I think I've paid for what I did or what I knew." She was resentenced to life without parole. But her days behind bars were numbered.

Faye Copeland, eighty-one, suffered a stroke on August 10, 2002, that left her partially paralyzed and unable to speak. She won a medical parole a few weeks later to a nursing home in Chillicothe, and she died there on December 30, 2003.

Her death provided a bookend for one of the most peculiar serial killing cases in Missouri history—or anywhere else, for that matter. There are more than a few people around tidy, industrious Chillicothe who believe that the bodies of other Copeland victims—perhaps those from the missing year of 1987—lie waiting to be discovered somewhere in the fertile farm soil of northern Missouri.

CHAPTER 8

Ricky and Dena,
the Snuff Film Killers

On a perfectly lovely May afternoon in 2006, an ex-convict named Ricky Davis left his apartment in Independence, Missouri, and pointed his blue Toyota east on Truman Road, the town's main drag. The gleaming skyline of Kansas City—ten miles distant—was in his rearview mirror a few blocks later as he passed the stately Victorian home where Harry Truman, the plain-spoken president who defined Independence, spent most of his life.

Davis continued east through downtown, then out past the vast power plant and across Highway 78, where Kansas City's sprawl finally gives way to soybean fields. Davis motored along a winding ridge, passing rural subdivisions that yielded to small homes, then trailers, then horses and cows.

He reached his destination, twenty miles from home, when he crossed a rusting green iron bridge over Sni-A-Bar Creek, at the twisting junction of two blacktop roads with utilitarian names: FF and D. He pulled off the road, retrieved a shovel from the trunk, and then walked down into a gnarly stand of maple trees, drooping and scrawny from the creek's frequent floods. There, Ricky Davis jabbed his shovel into the crusty soil and dug a hole big enough for a small body.

That same evening, a fisherman named Jack McGhee happened upon the freshly dug hole, which had nothing but a shovel inside. There was no sign of the digger. McGhee thought it was odd. He left the site alone and went on with his fishing. But he had a niggling unease about the hole, and he returned to the spot the next day. By then it had been filled in and obscured with tree limbs. Using a stick as a tool, McGhee began poking and scraping at the freshly turned soil. He stopped when, nine inches from the surface, he exposed a human hand. McGhee hurried to nearby Bates City to alert the police chief, Tim McCorkle. The chief confirmed the fisherman's find and summoned the Lafayette County sheriff's crime scene investigators.

The body belonged to Marsha Spicer, forty-one, a waiflike, 4-foot-11 woman from Kansas City. An autopsy showed an assortment of injuries. She had been choked a number of times, probably over many hours, but that was not the cause of death. Pathologist Thomas Gill determined that she was killed by suffocation or smothering, where a hand or some other object is held over the victim's mouth and nose, cutting off oxygen. Her body bore traces of cocaine and the sedative Trazodone. Gill also noted a postmortem head wound. He reasoned that she had been dropped, perhaps while being transported for burial. The pigment of the skin was wrong, and the corpse smelled like a laundry room. Gill concluded that someone had soaked Spicer's body in bleach.

Police in the Kansas City area were acquainted with Spicer, who some years before had succumbed to a lifestyle of narcotics and their attendant crime, prostitution. She lived at East 9th Street and

Van Brunt Boulevard, a rugged little corner of northeast Kansas City. A friend of Spicer, Emily Milburn, described it to me as a "twisted neighborhood" populated by men and women lost in the city's crack, meth, and OxyContin scene. Milburn told me that Spicer was a loving, caring friend in a crowd of "drugged-up fools." She rued what her life had become, and she tried to steer Milburn toward a different path.

"She told me that the drug game wasn't something I wanted to be involved with," Milburn said. "The people can't be trusted and no one is ever as nice as they seem. She seemed worried about me . . . She knew the game. She knew it was dangerous. She warned me not to get in deep."

Milburn recalled a heart-to-heart talk they had.

"She sat on my couch and cried about her life," she said. "The following day was her son's birthday, and her son's wife didn't want to have anything to do with Marsha. She was devastated."

On May 17, Detective Donald Hammond from Lafayette County, where Spicer's body was found, paid a visit to the building where Spicer had lived. A neighbor, Lorie Dunfield, provided information that began to reveal an appalling tale of violent sexual perversion that led back to Ricky Davis, the ex-con from Independence. Dunfield said Davis had phoned her three months before at the suggestion of his cousin, Athena Fagan. Davis told Dunfield he was interested in "sexual things"—not just sex, but "sexual things." Dunfield was willing, and she soon found herself in Davis's third-floor apartment in a regal old Tudor-style building on Independence's main drag. Their foreplay was kinky: Davis played a homemade videotape that showed him in a sexual threesome with his cousin Fagan and another woman. Dunfield and Davis had sex, and during pillow talk he invited her to join him in acting out his fantasy to create sexual snuff films.

"He wanted to have sex with a woman while she was giving oral sex [to another woman] and to choke her out or to suffocate her from behind," Dunfield told Detective Hammond. And he wanted to preserve it all on videotape for future entertainment. Dunfield said she declined to participate. But she also declined to report to police the fact that she had been solicited to join in a game of sexual murder. That decision would have consequences.

Dunfield directed the detective to Davis's apartment, and that evening Hammond and two Independence cops knocked at his door. Davis invited them into the apartment, where they found his girlfriend, a weathered-looking woman named Dena Riley, running around wearing nothing but underpants. The cops urged her to dress, and then had a look around. In the bedroom, Independence police sergeant Ed Turner noticed a video camera pointed at the bed. In the living room, Officer George Poletis saw an open journal with scribbled notes that included the words "choke," "victim," and "sexual." The details fit Dunfield's story. Hammond asked Davis to come "clear things up" at police headquarters. He declined to do so before consulting a lawyer, so the officers decided to secure the apartment and seek a search warrant. They told Davis and Riley to leave. A friend picked them up, and they drove off as the clutch of officers stood outside their apartment, waiting for authorization to go back inside.

Exactly 357 days before, Richard Dean Davis had been released from the Missouri prison across the state in Bonne Terre, after having spent seventeen years and eleven months locked up for sexual assault. He was at a crossroads that day, finally free after spending most of his life since puberty behind a locked door. Davis could have gone straight. But he would prove to be incapable of decency, of uprightness. He turned left instead.

Davis was born July 9, 1964, one of four children of a couple who split up as he was entering first grade. Davis grew up in northeast Kansas City in a cobbled-together stepfamily. Psychologist Steven Mandracchia would later describe Davis's childhood as "laden with pretty harsh physical abuse, inconstant adult figures and sexual abuse." He fought with his stepfather, Stan Cothern, whom Davis identified as one of several relatives who sexually abused him. When Davis was six years old, an aunt set up "simulated sexual acts" between him and his sister. The woman also regaled Davis with stories of her own sexual exploits.

By age ten, Davis was a chronic runaway and truant, and he dropped out altogether and left home as a seventh-grader, flopping with friends or living on the streets. In his adolescence, he spent three different stretches in the Western Missouri Mental Health Center, where he was diagnosed as depressed, angry, and anxious. "His anger and his sexuality became associated," Mandracchia said. He developed deviant fetishes—the clinical term is "paraphilia"—involving children and aggressive sex. From ages thirteen to seventeen, Davis spent most of his time in Missouri juvenile facilities for theft and other petty crimes. He was freed in 1982, just before his eighteenth birthday. Society soon learned that the troubled, deviant youngster had grown into a troubled, deviant adult—paranoid, antisocial, narcissistic, sexually violent.

Kathryn Seifert, a psychotherapist and author, told me that no one should have been surprised. Davis's childhood was a template for psychopaths and sociopaths, a topic explored in Seifert's book *How Children Become Violent*. "People don't just wake up one day and say, 'I'm going to be a serial rapist and a killer,'" Seifert said. "Something leads up to it."

She said kids raised like Davis "do not learn to attach to other people or develop relationships that teach them how what they do affects another person. They get stuck in a 'me-me-me' stage. That's normal when you're two. But that's not normal when you're twenty-two."

Davis had difficulties adjusting to freedom. He worked a series of minimum-wage jobs around Kansas City, but none lasted longer than a few weeks. Each time he was fired he had a dramatic explanation of how his failure was not his fault. In fact, Richard Davis proved to be one of those deeply flawed people who is simply unable to function as a productive member of society. And the depth of his flaws would become ever more apparent.

Unable to maintain a job, Davis turned to crime, but he was no better at that. In 1984, authorities in and around Kansas City bundled a series of unrelated charges against him—larceny, breaking and entering, receiving stolen property—into a single prosecution.

Convicted and sentenced to three years in prison, he served twenty-six months and was paroled in April 1986. Still just twenty-one years old, he hadn't learned much. Freedom once again would prove fleeting.

In October 1987, a woman driving near Lexington, Missouri, stopped to help Davis as he stood on a road beside a car with its hood up. The Samaritan was a twenty-seven-year-old woman. Davis bummed a ride, then pulled a knife and directed the woman to a deserted spot, where he raped, sodomized, and beat her. Identified though his broken-down car, Davis first claimed the sex was consensual, then changed his story and pleaded guilty, banking on a lenient sentence. Instead, he was locked up for a month shy of eighteen years.

Davis claimed to have found God in prison. He avowed his new-found faith to the parole board, and he swore he would walk the line henceforth. It was all a con. The 5-foot-11 Missourian was loosed on society with bulging prison-yard muscles and a singular mission to experience the ultimate form of sexual domination: murder through sadistic asphyxiation. He began frequent visits to strangulation fetish websites and masturbated over videos featuring sado-masochistic role-playing. He was obsessed with the Oliver Stone film *Natural Born Killers*, in which lovers Mickey and Mallory commit murders for kicks.

Davis imagined himself as Mickey. But he needed a Mallory. He found her at work. After prison, Davis found employment as a janitor as a Kansas City metal fabrication factory. Dena Riley was hired there part-time in January 2006. Days after they met, Riley and Davis were living together on Truman Road in Independence.

Dena Delores Riley, thirty-eight, was a buxom woman with bad teeth and a meth jones. She grew up in Kansas City and married straight out of Hickman Hills High School in 1985. She and her husband had three kids in five years. By the birth of the third, Dena was bored. "She got tired of being a mom," her husband, Mark Riley, told the *Kansas City Star*. "She felt she missed out, because she got married right out of high school." While she caught up on sex and drugs, her husband got a divorce and custody of the children. Over the next fifteen years, from 1990 until she met Ricky Davis, Riley lived at the edges of Kansas City. Terminally addicted to one narcotic or another, she bounced between short-term jobs, dabbled in prostitution, and spent time in jail and on the streets.

Davis and Riley took different routes to arrive at the same depraved place, and it was a match made in hell.

Ricky Davis considered himself a playboy, and he hit on nearly every woman he met. He had brown hair (his prison mullet hairdo was later shorn short), hazel eyes, a scruffy mustache, a cleft turtle chin, and a collection of bad jailhouse tattoos. He was so obviously an ex-con that he might as well have had his prison I.D. number stamped on his forehead. His relentlessly pursued a downstairs neighbor in Independence, and her take on Davis indicates that he was an agile con; she later said he seemed like "a real nice guy." Her instincts needed honing.

Davis shared his sexual fantasies with Riley. She was willing, and the two began trawling the grimy edges of Kansas City for prospective participants in his snuff fetish. They began videotaping their own sex and threesomes with meth-addicted women who subjected themselves to violent, demeaning, and dangerous sex in exchange for a high. Davis was bold enough—or naïve enough—to spell out his snuff-sex threesome fantasy for Lorie Dunfield, Marsha Spicer's neighbor. She opted "to get the heck out of there," as she put it. But Dena Riley didn't.

The couple's first sexual guinea pig was Michelle Ricci, thirty-six. Once an attractive brunette, Ricci had fallen into meth addiction and prostitution. Davis apparently picked her up on the street in late April 2006, and they made a deal to exchange a few hours of sex for narcotics. Instead, she was held at the Independence apartment for several days and used a sadomasochistic sex object. Ricci was subjected to rape, bondage, torture, and choking. Davis videotaped portions of the assaults. Ricci, her wrists bound with yellow speaker wire, is seen on the tape with a crimson face and a vein bulging on her forehead. She had just been choked to near death, and she looked mortified.

Davis and Riley experimented with Ricci in bringing to life his fantasy of watching Riley smother another woman by sitting on her face. She proved unable to finish the job with her groin. After holding Ricci for seventy-two hours, the lovers feared she would go to police. They decided to kill her. Davis drove her in his Toyota into secluded woods near Highways 210 and 291 in Clay County, south of Liberty and north of the Missouri River. He forced her to disrobe, and then tried to strangle her with a rope garrote. When she failed to die, he suffocated Ricci by covering her mouth and nostrils with his bare hands. Davis left the nude body covered with debris and branches. Concerned about DNA evidence, he returned the next day, doused Ricci's body with lighter fluid and set it afire. It lay undetected there for nearly a month.

The thrill of the sexual murder satiated Davis for a few weeks, but by mid-May he needed another fix. Davis had become acquainted with tiny Marsha Spicer about six weeks earlier, apparently meeting on the street in Lorie Dunfield's neighborhood. It's not clear whether they had had sex previously, but on May 14 they made a sex-for-meth deal. He drove her home to Independence, where Dena Riley was waiting. Davis got things rolling by feeding Spicer a handful of Vicodin pills, a pain reliever.

For the ensuing thirty-six hours, Riley and Davis sexually abused Marsha Spicer in every way imaginable, and they made a graphic record of their abuse in three videotapes. The tapes show Spicer being subjected to various forms of sexual penetration. They show Davis choking her and both Davis and Riley punching her. The tapes also show Riley repeatedly sitting on Spicer's face in an attempt to suffocate her, sometimes while Davis is having vaginal sex with the woman. Riley did finally succeed in suffocating Spicer with her crotch. The tape shows Davis and Riley kissing passionately over Spicer's limp body.

Moments after the murder, Dena Riley rolled out of bed, went to Davis's computer, and began playing the "Pogo" video game. Riley later said that she was unaware Spicer was dead and that she and Davis argued about what they had done. Davis admitted that they had "fucked up." Just as in the murder of Michelle Ricci, Davis became obsessed with disposing of the DNA the two had left in and on Spicer's body. He carried the victim to the bathtub, covered her body with water, and then poured in a gallon of bleach.

Davis and Riley did not exactly collapse with remorse. While Spicer's body spent ten hours soaking in the bleached water, Davis and Riley attended a high school graduation party for one of his nephews. Later, he drove east out of Independence so he could dig the hole at Sni-A-Bar Creek, where he had fished as a kid. At midnight that night, he drained the tub and wrapped Spicer's remains in plastic and an old rug. He dropped the corpse while carrying it down the long flight of stairs behind their apartment. He returned to the creek, dropped her body in the hole, then covered it. The next day, he and Riley drove to her mom's house to celebrate Mother's Day.

But the gig was up for the killers when Spicer's body was found by the fisherman and cops turned up at their door in Independence. It took two trips before a judge to secure a warrant to search the apartment. When they finally got back inside, investigators found a stomach-turning, two-hour videotape that showed Spicer—her eyes covered with duct tape at times—being raped and strangled.

"They did the tape because they enjoyed watching it," Jackson County Prosecutor Michael Sanders told reporters. "It was in the machine when we got there. They had been watching it."

They found a second tape that showed their assault on Michelle Ricci—a crime that police had not been aware of because her body had not been found and she had not been reported missing.

By the time the apartment was being searched, Davis and Riley were on the lam in a friend's borrowed pickup truck. They knew they were busted. Missouri authorities issued a bulletin for their apprehension, and the snuff-film killers suddenly became national news.

Overnight, the couple had gone from obscure perverts to "America's Most Wanted." Authorities tracked them via their cell phone calls and credit card purchases. They wandered east to St. Louis, then south to Perryville, Missouri, where Riley had a friend, Susan Summers. They told her they had "raped and killed a lady" and planned "to go somewhere and kill themselves." They backtracked to Kansas City to buy meth, then made their way south and across the state line into Arcadia, Kansas, where they turned up at the home of Davis's stepsister and her husband, parents of a five-year-old girl. Davis made an elaborate display of his newfound Christianity for his kin, who apparently hadn't been watching the news.

The next day, May 25, the stepsister allowed Davis and Riley to go for lunch with the niece. When they didn't return, she called police and learned that the couple was wanted for the sex murders. Davis and Riley each sexually assaulted the child while driving back roads along the Kansas-Missouri border.

They then planned suicide. Each swallowed a handful of pills. Davis decided the child deserved mercy. He planned to drop her outside her home in Arcadia, then race away to a remote spot, where he and his lover would embrace, drift off to sleep, and die of overdoses—Romeo and Juliet on meth. But they were too high to find their way back to Arcadia.

Davis used his cell phone to call 911 in Barton County, Kansas, at about 4:30 P.M., five hours after the abduction. He sought directions, explaining he wanted to free the child before committing suicide because "we've done a lot of bad things." Deputy Vincent Ashworth had the groggy Davis on the phone for twenty minutes, keeping him conscious to try to preserve the little girl beside him. Riley finally blurted out the name on a road sign, and deputies raced in that direction. They arrived a few minutes after Davis had run the truck in a ditch. He was trying to push the truck back on the road, and the child—her shorts covered in blood—was sitting safely in the truck of a farmer who happened by. Riley had a broken nose. Davis was not hurt. They were arrested for murder and more. The niece underwent surgery for damage from the brutal rape.

Authorities back in Independence were left to try to explain why Davis and Riley were allowed to walk away while the search warrant was being sought. These did not strike the local police and county sheriff as legitimate inquiries. They were both stunningly defensive. "You can spin the facts any way you want," said Independence Police Chief Fred Mills. "Hindsight is a wonderful thing," added Lafayette County Sheriff Kerrick Alumbaugh.

Davis and Riley cooperated after their arrest. Each gave a detailed confession, and Davis led authorities to Ricci's body in Clay County. He also gave up a trove of additional videotapes, including two more featuring the assault on Spicer, that he had hidden at the plant where he worked. Authorities feared more victims might turn up, but none did.

The prosecutors with jurisdiction vowed to seek the death penalty. "The most vile and criminal act should be subject to the ultimate punishment," said Daniel White of Clay County. Added Jackson County Prosecutor Mike Sanders, "There is no negotiation at that point. . . The crime was wanton, vile, and inhuman."

In August 2008, Davis faced trial in Jackson County for the murder of Spicer. It was not a difficult prosecution; Davis's confession and the videotapes provided graphic evidence of the horrors he had committed. He was convicted on twenty-three felony counts. In his testimony during the penalty phase, Davis was contrite but also was reflective enough to acknowledge that an apology was "lame" after his vile acts.

"I know I'm a bad person," Davis said. "I don't care about anybody. I don't care about myself. And other times I hate that I care so much. I'm sorry. . . I don't know what to say."

The jury chose not to show mercy. It recommended death, and Judge Marco Roldan condemned Davis to die by lethal injection. He joined about fifty other Death Row inmates at Potosi state prison in Mineral Point, Missouri.

Four months later, Dena Riley was allowed to plead guilty in exchange for a terminal prison sentence. For the Spicer murder she got life without parole for the homicide and additional long sentences for sodomy, kidnapping, and sexual abuse. For the Ricci murder she got five additional consecutive life sentences for forcible sodomy and add-on sentences for sexual abuse, assault, and felonious restraint. She also pleaded guilty to federal kidnapping charges in the child's abduction and got yet another term of life without parole. In all, she is serving nine consecutive life sentences behind the walls of the state prison in Chillicothe.

Years before he was caught, Dennis Rader, the infamous "BTK Killer" in the Wichita, Kansas, area, sent a letter to a TV station in which he suggested that sexual psychopaths—men like himself, Ted Bundy, and Jack the Ripper—have what he called "factor x." He wrote, "There is no help, no cure, except death or being caught and put away."

I asked Kathryn Seifert, the psychotherapist, whether Rader was on to something. She said, "He knew he had this drive to kill and hurt, and he knew that it was something that the rest of the world didn't have. . . Psychopaths have no empathy. They get a thrill out of hurting people. That is what sets them apart from run-of-the-mill sociopaths."

And that describes Richard Davis. Raised amid unthinkable abuse, he became an unconscionable, inhumane abuser. He was branded with "factor x."

CHAPTER 9

Lust and Greed on the Cul-de-Sac

It was one of those murders that made no sense.

At six o'clock on the evening of December 27, 1997, Richard Abeln, a St. Louis transportation executive, stopped at the office of his aviation firm at St. Louis Downtown Airport, just across the Mississippi River in Cahokia, Illinois. Seated beside Abeln in his manly GMC Yukon was Debra, forty-four, his wife of twenty-three years. In the backseat was the youngest of their three sons, Travis, age eleven.

The Abelns were planning to meet their older sons for a post-Christmas dinner that Saturday evening, but Richard told his wife that he had to make a quick stop at the airport office to see about work that had been done on his small private airplane. As they arrived there, a masked man brandishing a stubby shotgun confronted the family in the SUV. He opened the passenger's side front door—where Debra Abeln was seated—and demanded their valuables. The Abelns did all the right things. They quickly complied, passing the robber their jewelry and cash.

It should have been a simple criminal transaction—a routine armed robbery of the sort that happens hundreds of times across America every day: Take the money and run. But the man trained his gun on Debra Abeln at point-blank range and fired two shots directly into her chest. Only then did he run to a sedan parked nearby and flee as the life drained out of the body of the wife and mother.

Travis Abeln used the car phone to place a frantic call to 911. Richard Abeln then phoned his oldest son, Ryan, who was waiting for them at a restaurant, to let him know that his mother had been shot and killed by a robber. Authorities arrived and found Richard Abeln in a state of hysteria. Why, he pleaded. Why?

It was a legitimate question.

"Police officers tell people to always cooperate when they find themselves in situations like this," Sgt. Dennis Kuba of the Illinois State Police told the *St. Louis Post-Dispatch*. "She did everything she possibly could and answered all of his demands. For whatever reason, he decided to shoot her anyway."

If the killer was worried about witnesses, why not shoot all three victims? If he fired out of fear, why not shoot the father, a menacing physical specimen at 6-foot-3 and 220 pounds? Why was Debra Abeln singled out?

The venue of the robbery was another puzzler. The small corporate airport was an unlikely place for a random stickup on a quiet Saturday evening. There hadn't been a violent crime there in its history. The local police chief dubbed the crime "strange." The airport director called it "off the wall." It was as though the robber was expecting Richard and Debra Abeln that night.

The Abelns were not exactly the Rockefellers, but they lived a comfortable life. The high school sweethearts had three sons: Ryan, twenty-one, Chad, fifteen, and Travis, eleven. They lived in a stately brick home on a cul-de-sac in Sappington, Missouri, a well-heeled St. Louis suburb in South County. Richard Abeln had built a six-figure income in the transportation business. He owned CRT Aviation, an aircraft hangar and refueling and maintenance firm. But the jewel of his holdings was Jeffco Leasing, a one hundred–employee trucking firm based in St. Louis that was estimated to be worth $17 million.

As with any murder investigation, police began by scrutinizing those closest to the victim, including her spouse. At a glance, they seemed to be a perfect fit as a couple. Richard stayed very busy with work while Debra dedicated herself to raising their sons. But the probe soon turned up evidence that the marriage was not all that it seemed to be.

The Yukon had been impounded as crime-scene evidence, and investigators made an interesting discovery as they began poring over the vehicle. They found Richard Abeln's briefcase in the car. And inside, they found love notes to him written by a woman named Cindy Baur. The investigation began and ended with the husband. Police quickly discerned that Abeln was a serial philanderer who was sneaking around on both Baur and his wife.

Detectives also discovered that Abeln had a curiously close relationship with another businessman, Guy Westmoreland, thirty-five, who operated a gas station adjacent to Jeffco headquarters at the edge of downtown St. Louis. Jeffco bought fuel from Westmoreland under contract. The men proved to be in obsessively constant contact. Phone records showed that Abeln and Westmoreland exchanged thirty-six calls in the last nine days of December, including ten on December 26, the day before Debra Abeln was killed. Westmoreland's phone records also showed 155 calls over the previous few months with a resident of Edinburg, Texas, near the Mexican border. Authorities in the Lone Star State suggested a drug-smuggling link.

On January 5, Richard Abeln and his son Ryan agreed to travel to an Illinois State Police office, ostensibly to discuss posting a reward in the case. With a list of questions about Abeln's affairs, the state of his marriage, and his ties to Westmoreland and narcotics, police invited Abeln to take a lie detector test—a formality, the state detectives told him. But he failed miserably, and over the ensuing eighteen hours, Richard Abeln admitted that he was responsible for his wife's murder.

Detectives broke the news to Ryan Abeln, the eldest son.

"My first reaction was, 'No, that's impossible. Something's wrong,'" Ryan Abeln later said. But his father soon confirmed the despicable truth in a conversation with Ryan late on the night of his confession. "I'm sorry I ruined your lives," the father said through crocodile tears.

Guy Westmoreland was very interested in the events that day. He beeped Ryan Abeln nearly ten times, seeking updates on the visit to police. Within ninety minutes of signing his confession, Richard Abeln phoned Westmoreland, with police recording the conversation. He tried to draw him out as a co-conspirator, saying police were suspicious about them. But Westmoreland replied that the cops were bluffing and that Abeln should call a lawyer immediately. Based on Abeln's confession, police used a warrant the following day and found 550 grams of cocaine in Westmoreland's GMC Suburban.

The nut was cracked.

In the rich human history of love triangle murders, the combination of lust and greed has served as primary motivator in countless instances. And the killers almost never get away with it. Richard Abeln should have done some research, read the literature.

Abeln's mistress, Cindy Baur, admitted that she had carried on a fifteen-month affair with the married man. She said they occasionally engaged in post-coital reveries about making their relationship legitimate. But each time the subject came up, Abeln would wring his hands over the potential loss of half his assets, the downside of divorce. So instead, he decided to exchange his soul for ephemeral wealth—and invited his young son along as a witness to his own mother's murder. Five minutes before the murder, Abeln was laughing and joking with his wife and son. He seemed to be in a very good mood, Travis later said.

"It's horrible enough for a guy to have this done to his wife," Patrick Delaney, an Illinois police official, told reporters. "But in front of your eleven-year-old son? It's just going to scar him for life."

Abeln was a man involved in serial affairs, a drug-smuggling scheme, and god knows what other immoralities and illegalities. Yet he was so filled with hubris that he convinced himself that he could get away with it—that police scrutiny would not ferret out his guilt, even as he left love letters at the scene of the crime. It turned out that he overestimated himself. Richard Abeln made it eminently clear that he had more testosterone than brains.

In his confession, Abeln admitted that he and Guy Westmoreland had become partners in a drug scheme in the spring of 1997, nine months before the murder. Westmoreland had the south Texas connections, and Abeln provided the airplanes. It was a rinky-dink operation—a few kilos. Four times, a pilot named Tony Jestis, who worked for Abeln, flew to south Texas to buy Mexican cocaine, a kilo at a time, from Ronnie Gray of Edinburg. (Investigators said the men marked themselves as drug pikers by paying Gray as much as $16,000 a kilo, forty percent over the going rate.) Westmoreland would break the kilos into one-ounce packages and sell them in St. Louis. Even at the inflated price they paid, the men doubled their money, earning $32,000 a kilo in street sales.

Westmoreland was no saint, but Abeln used deception to draw him into the contract murder plan. He lied and told Westmoreland that his wife had discovered the drug scheme and was threatening to go to police. Westmoreland had his own dose of hubris. He liked to brag, for example, about his crime bona fides. As Ryan Abeln later testified about Westmoreland, "He said, 'If you need anybody killed, I'll kill them for $1,000.' You could be talking about the weather, and he would say he could have someone killed."

The triggerman he hired for the Abeln job was not so professional. He was DeAndre Lewis, twenty-four, who worked pumping gas at Westmoreland's St. Louis filling station. He agreed to kill Debra Abeln in exchange for five ounces of cocaine, worth about $5,000 retail. On December 17, 1997, Westmoreland and Lewis lurked outside the offices of Abeln's aviation company. The woman arrived there after sunset, summoned on a ruse by her husband. But Lewis could not manage to get off a good shot in the dark. The murder plot succeeded on its second go-round ten days later.

After Abeln's confession, he and the others alleged to be involved in the smuggling and murder—Jestis, Gray, Lewis, and Westmoreland—were charged with federal crimes. (Both the narcotics case and the homicide involved the crossing of state borders for criminal purposes.)

Richard Abeln transferred his assets to his sons, asked for a court-appointed lawyer, and eventually pleaded guilty in May 1999. Through more tears, a trembling Abeln managed to mutter a simple "yes" when a judge asked whether he had conspired to kill his wife. In exchange for testimony against the other conspirators, he was spared a death sentence and got life without parole—although the sentence would prove irrelevant.

Triggerman DeAndre Lewis also pleaded guilty to murder, avoiding a possible death sentence and gaining a prison term that gave him the possibility of parole. His scheduled release date is in 2033, when he would be fifty-six years old. Pilot Jestis and Ronnie Gray, the Texas man who supplied the cocaine, each were convicted on drug charges and served less than five years in prison.

Westmoreland was charged with conspiracy to distribute narcotics. He was not charged with the murder, per se. He was vacationing in Florida at the time of the slaying—"conveniently," as an appeals court judge put it—and federal prosecutors decided to focus on the drug charge. But that trial became a by-default homicide hearing. Much of the testimony centered on the slaying of Debra Abeln, and the witnesses against him included Richard Abeln and his sons Ryan and Travis. Richard Abeln testified that he had never seriously considered murdering his wife until Westmoreland convinced him how easy it would be to hire a killer.

Cindy Baur, Abeln's mistress, took the stand as a defense witness. Her testimony gave a glimpse of the stunning gullibility of a woman who spent fifteen months engaged sexually with a married man. She said she had been unaware of Abeln's other side romances until she was clued in by detectives. Yet, Baur said, she had remained in contact with Abeln, who continued to assure her that he was not involved in his wife's murder—even after he had pleaded guilty to killing her.

Westmoreland was convicted on August 20, 1998, and sentenced to life without possibility of parole because the judge was allowed under federal guidelines to use the murder as an aggravating circumstance. He did not go away quietly, pressing a series of appeals to little avail. (A court appeals panel ordered a new sentence based upon a trial error, but Westmoreland got the same punishment the second time around: life without parole.) He was convicted in 2001 on a series of additional federal charges in connection with the case, including use of interstate commerce facilities to commit murder for hire; conspiracy to commit murder for hire; tampering with a witness by committing murder; and causing the death of a witness through use of a firearm. At last word, he was a middle-aged man serving out the rest of his life at the federal penitentiary in Terre Haute, Indiana.

And what of Richard Abeln? In the end, he did prove to have some glimmer of a conscience. He could not live with what he had done.

In September 1998, he survived a suicide attempt after slashing a wrist and his groin with a razor blade at a county jail in Illinois. He proved to be persistent in his pursuit of death, attempting various methods of suicide over the next several years, often leaving self-pitying notes. On December 29, 2002, five years and two days after witnessing his wife's murder, he tried again. He twisted his prison uniform into a noose and hanged himself from the window bars in his cell at the federal penitentiary in Pollock, Louisiana. It finally worked. He was gone for good, at age forty-eight.

CHAPTER 10

Meacham Park's
Angry Cookie Goes Off

Chuck Runnels answered a knock at his door on the afternoon of February 7, 2008, and found his old pal Charles Thornton standing at the threshold.

Runnels invited Thornton into his home there in the old inner-ring St. Louis suburb of Kirkwood, and the men sat together for more than an hour. They chatted, watched TV, ate a sandwich, and then Thornton finally got around to the point of his visit. Runnels and Thornton were board members of the Men's Breakfast Club, a benevolent group that donated to charitable causes in their neighborhood, Meacham Park, the traditionally black section of Kirkwood. Thornton asked his friend to look after a file filled with materials from the men's group, including a small amount of cash and a photo album. He didn't explain why, and Runnels didn't ask.

Runnels assumed Thornton was going away to Florida, as he frequently did. When that business was completed, Thornton stood to leave. He exited with his life-is-good smile and his signature phrase: "Glory be to God."

He didn't say so, but Thornton was marching off to settle a score.

Charles Thornton, known to everyone as Cookie, was born two days before Christmas in 1955. He grew up in a big family in Meacham Park, the orphan black neighborhood that clings like a barnacle to the south tip of Kirkwood, tucked in against a bend in Interstate 44. The neighborhood's street names became Kirkwood code words for ghetto: Orleans, New York, Chicago, Memphis.

Thornton was a Meacham Park success story, a talented black athlete who stood out in several sports at Kirkwood High. In particular, he excelled at two track specialties, the high jump and the triple jump, events that often attract the best athletes because they combine speed, power, and agility. Thornton was the Missouri state champion in both events in 1973 and 1974. After high school, he won a track scholarship to Northeast Missouri State University in Kirksville (now Truman State). He was a track standout in college as well, breaking school records in his specialties. As a senior in 1979, he was named a small-college All-American in both the high jump and triple jump. His accomplishments made him a fixture in the St. Louis sport pages.

Thornton returned to Meacham Park a conquering hero after college. He had a bachelor's degree in business administration, and he seemed destined for prosperity, with his athlete's work ethic and can-do disposition. Ask him how he was doing, and he would enthuse, "*fan*-tastic!" God came up at the beginning or end of nearly every conversation—a tendency he inherited from his mother, Annie Bell Thornton: "God bless," he would say, as both hello and goodbye.

Young Thornton went to work in the construction trades, learning the building business inside-out—everything from demolition, remodeling, and new construction to landscaping and paving. He was soon doing his own side jobs, and in 1987, at age thirty-one, Thornton made his business legitimate, registering his construction firm under the name Cookco. The following year, his personal life aligned with the apparent fortunes of his professional life. He married Marilyn Thomas, and three years later their daughter, Sarah, was born. It seemed as though Cookie Thornton had everything a man could want.

When Thornton was growing up, déclassé Meacham Park, with its tiny shotgun shacks on twenty-five-foot-wide lots, was adjacent to but distinctly apart from Kirkwood, with its massive Italianate and Victorian homes and generous yards. Kirkwood (population 30,000) has always held itself in high regard, the self-designated "Queen of the St. Louis Suburbs." It was a railroad town created by the Missouri Pacific, and its lovely stone train station, dating to 1893, is the soul of its boutique-lined downtown. Its namesake was James Kirkwood, the man who designed the railroad through the town. A century ago, Kirkwood proclaimed itself "rich in all that is good," a city "free from contaminating influences, and where the best advantages are had for the bringing up of Young America."

And then there was Meacham Park—so close, yet so far away. The neighborhood was founded about 1900 when a Memphis businessman, Elzey Meacham, carved up 158 acres into a grid of two dozen dirt streets. It was intended from the beginning as a home for African Americans, and it became one of those turkey scratch hamlets where nearly every home had a big garden, chickens, and maybe a hog or two. It reached a zenith after World War II, with a population of more than one thousand, served by a half-dozen churches.

Although it was surrounded by thriving modern suburbs, Meacham Park lacked decent sewer and water service until the late 1960s, when St. Louis County finally made improvements with federal grant money. Even during the American annexation fever of the 1960s and '70s, Meacham Park was viewed as a tax liability, and it remained an unincorporated part of the county. For decades, Kirkwood wanted no part of Meacham Park. Paul Ward, the second black man ever elected to Kirkwood City Council, told me that Meacham Park served as the county's "dumping ground" for subsidized housing. He added, "And we all know what that means."

That changed in the late 1980s, when annexation suddenly seemed advantageous to Kirkwood. By then, Meacham Park was a social trough, with entrenched crime, drug problems, and an increasingly dilapidated housing stock. It wasn't benevolence that prompted Kirkwood's annexation interest. Meacham Park became desirable because the county decided that its location at a busy I-44 interchange was perfect for a big-box shopping mall. Meacham Park's residents found themselves being courted. After a series of meetings, reports, and promises, voters in both Kirkwood and Meacham Park gave their approval, and in 1991 the orphan neighborhood finally had a municipal big brother.

The city found a developer (or a series of them) and used condemnation powers to level homes and other buildings on 55 acres to make way for a new mall complex—Kirkwood Commons and several adjacent properties, totaling more than 500,000 square feet of retail space—at the formerly scruffy western edge of Meacham Park. The neighborhood became a construction zone. Sixty-two displaced residents got new homes, and many other homeowners were given as much as $37,000 in forgivable loans to improve their properties. The county renovated thirty-five public housing units. A gated townhouse development went up. A nursing home was built nearby.

The construction work and retail outlets were said to add as many as seven hundred jobs in the neighborhood, and the various firms involved were encouraged to practice "First Source" hiring—meaning from the neighborhood, with a special focus on minority enterprises. As owner of Cookco, Cookie Thornton was well-positioned to capitalize on this $100 million transformation. It was his neighborhood. He felt a personal stake. Early on, Cookco got a few small demolition contracts. He knocked down a couple of houses and did some paving work. He earned less than $100,000 but was inspired to buy a new dump truck and other expensive equipment, expecting much more work. It didn't work out that way.

"They promised him a larger role, and he didn't get what he was promised," his brother Arthur Thornton, younger by ten years, later told reporters. "He was the only contractor from the neighborhood. One of the promises was that they were going to give work to people living in the neighborhood and the contractors in the neighborhood."

Thornton's life began to turn in 1993. He split with his wife that year, with their daughter still just a toddler. In 1995 he married Maureen Sutherlin, a school teacher and administrator. They had a nontraditional relationship, living one thousand miles apart after she took a job as a school principal near Tampa. Friends noticed that happy-go-lucky Cookie began growing edgy. He grumbled about politicians and bureaucrats, who he believed were holding him back financially. In fact, Thornton lost out on development contracts because he was lousy at putting together the voluminous paperwork required for competitive bids. City officials tried to help him, but he resisted. "He thought that he had special rights and privileges when it came to the work because he was from Meacham Park, and that was it," said Councilman Ward, a longtime friend of Thornton.

Thornton wasted money he didn't have by hiring an attorney to file a lawsuit alleging racism by the developer and his competitors. When that failed, he ran for Kirkwood City Council, hoping to gain an insider's advantage on contracts. He finished next-to-last in a six-person race. Thornton grew increasingly single-minded. Driven by a deepening financial despair, he began staging protests, using his dump truck to blockade construction sites.

Thornton owed the government $200,000 after failing to pay withholding taxes for six years, from 1992 to 1998. He owed nearly that much for the dump truck and other equipment. He owed his daughter's mother $10,000 in child support, and he was in arrears in rent for his Cookco "World Headquarters," as he jokingly called it. With debts of $500,000, he went bankrupt in 1999, and a judge devised a repayment plan of $4,425 a month. It was a pipe dream. Thornton's income was nowhere near that, and he defaulted immediately. Cookco was evicted. With nowhere to legally park his construction vehicles and store equipment, he resorted to using a lot across the street from his parents' Meacham Park home, where he slept in his boyhood bedroom. This seemingly innocuous decision would have dire consequences.

Kirkwood, like every municipality in America, has detailed codes that specify where and when commercial vehicles can be parked. Thornton began to amass citations for illegal parking and storage—fifty-eight tickets in 2000 and nearly that many in 2001, with fines ultimately surpassing $20,000 for some two hundred infractions. He couldn't afford to pay, of course. The futility of the situation was not lost on Kirkwood officials, some of whom quietly urged cops and enforcement officers to leave Thornton alone. But it was too late, from Cookie Thornton's perspective. He had decided that the city was out to get him. His focus became a single citation that listed the wrong address as the location of an ordinance violation. Thornton fought the ticket, pointing out the clear error. Ultimately, a judge ruled against him. Thornton was incensed.

Councilman Ward told me the incident was a turning point for Thornton, who grew convinced of a government conspiracy against him.

"He just believed he had found grounds that supported his side, and nothing was going to deter him," Ward said. "This became his central point of focus from that day forward. He dug in his heel. He said, 'They're picking on me. They were wrong and they won't admit that they were wrong.' And it just snowballed from there."

Thornton began showing up at Kirkwood council meetings to air his grievances. Like most gadflies with a beef, he was initially viewed as sad, somewhat comical, but harmless. But in the summer of 2001 he was charged with assault for a belligerent confrontation with Ken Yost, Kirkwood's public works director, whom Thornton believed was singling him out for enforcement. Thornton was convicted of misdemeanor assault. The case became an obsession as he sued in both state and federal courts for malicious prosecution. His final appeal in that case was finally dismissed in 2006, five years after it all began.

By then, he had embarked on a series of ill-considered deals that led his parents to financial ruin and put a wedge in his relationships with his two brothers, Gerald, two years older than Cookie, and Arthur. Using the power of attorney his parents had given him, Thornton had refinanced their Meacham Park home in 2003, taking $72,000 in equity from a residence they owned outright. Fourteen months later, he refinanced his parents' retirement home in Florida, taking $230,000 in equity. No one seems to know what he did with the money. He did not use it to pay off debts; he still owed the IRS $200,000 in 2007.

In the meantime, Thornton's reputation as an obsessed citizen continued to grow. In 2005, he was photographed by the media picketing outside the law office of Kirkwood City Attorney John Hessel. He wore a sandwich board that read, "Why oh why in Kirkwood are we treated like slaves again."

On May 18, 2006, Thornton was arrested and charged with disorderly conduct after he cast himself on the floor of the Kirkwood City Council chambers and refused to leave. He was arrested again four weeks later when he brayed like a donkey and chanted "jackass, jackass, jackass" for several minutes. The council considered banning Thornton, and city officials discussed whether they could or should compel him to get mental help. Mayor Mike Swoboda spoke about the council's Thornton problem at a June 1, 2006, meeting. "The City Council has decided that they will not lower themselves to Mr. Thornton's level," Swoboda said, according to the *Webster-Kirkwood Times*. "We will act with integrity and continue to deal with him at these council proceedings. However, we will not allow Mr. Thornton or any other person to disrupt these proceedings." Thornton responded by mockingly asking whether he would be allowed to use phrases such as "lame jackass" or "displaying the qualities of a jackass." Some Kirkwood officials tried to reason with Thornton.

"Every time I saw Cookie, I'd stop to talk to him," Police Chief Jack Plummer later told the *St. Louis Post-Dispatch*. "I was constantly trying to look for resolution. My big concern was that the obsessiveness of what he was doing was going to ruin his life."

Thornton was convicted and fined $2,000 for his council chamber antics. He turned to the courts in another quixotic quest for legal relief. He sued Kirkwood, seeking $14 million in damages for denial of his First Amendment right to speak at a public meeting. When a state lawsuit was dismissed, he began banking on a federal suit. At the same time he got more bad financial news: In January 2008, the Florida home he owned with his long-distance wife went into foreclosure. Worth $150,000, the home had been refinanced for twice that.

Cookie Thornton's coup de grâce came on January 28, 2008. The federal lawsuit, his last hope, was lost. U.S. District Court Judge Catherine Perry ruled that Thornton's constitutional rights had not been violated. She wrote, "Any restrictions on Thornton's speech were reasonable, viewpoint-neutral, and served important governmental interests." The judge added that Thornton "does not have a First Amendment right to engage in irrelevant debate and to voice repetitive, personal, virulent attacks against Kirkwood and its city officials."

Thornton was in tears when he phoned his friend Joe Cole to report the dismissal of his federal lawsuit.

"He was talking off the wall," Cole later told the *Post-Dispatch*. "He was sniffling and crying."

Thornton told Cole, "They aren't going to get away with this." He mentioned an upcoming council meeting—probably the only tip about what was to come. Cole said, "I just thought all he was going to do was go up to City Hall and throw chairs." But he planned so much more.

Ten days later, on February 7, Thornton stopped to see his friend Runnels to drop off materials from the neighborhood group. He then drove a couple of miles to Kirkwood's tidy downtown, arriving a few minutes before 7 P.M., the starting time of that night's city council meeting. He parked his car, tucked a revolver in his coat pocket, and marched toward City Hall.

On the way, he crossed paths with Kirkwood Police Sergeant William Biggs Jr., fifty. A twenty-year police veteran with a wife and two sons, Biggs had once worked as a rodeo cowboy, and he was looking forward to raising cattle after his retirement. Thornton approached Biggs, drew his gun, and shot and killed the cop. Thornton grabbed Biggs's .44-caliber police revolver and strode on, now armed with two guns.

Inside City Hall, some forty people were about to begin the routine business of running a small city. Those assembled included the eight council members, the mayor, city department heads, a couple of reporters, and a dozen citizens. They had just wrapped up the Pledge of Allegiance when Cookie Thornton arrived. Heads turned. There must have been some heavy sighs. Officer Tom Ballman, thirty-seven, a husband and father of two, a husky blond cop with nine years on the Kirkwood force, was the first to get in Thornton's path, just inside the door. Thornton shot the officer dead.

Thornton then marched purposefully toward the front of the chambers and the long, curved desk where council members and the mayor were seated. Some said Thornton chanted, "Shoot the mayor." But Janet McNichols, covering the meeting for the *Post-Dispatch*, said Thornton's first target seemed to be Ken Yost, the public works director who had become his scapegoat. He fired a fatal shot to Yost's head. Another clear target was City Attorney Hessel. The chamber was in chaos as Thornton stalked after Hessel, who saved his own life by throwing several plastic chairs at his attacker. He later said he looked Thornton in the eye and said, "Cookie, don't do this." Hessel escaped serious injury. Others were not so lucky. Mayor Mike Swoboda, Councilwoman Connie Karr, and Councilman Michael Lynch also were shot. Karr and Lynch died at the scene, and Mayor Swoboda, shot in the head, would linger seven months before dying. Todd Smith, a reporter for a suburban paper, was hit in the hand. Two police officers rushed into the room. Oddly, Thornton is said to have shouted, "I have a gun!" These were his last words. The officers opened fire, and the gadfly fell dead near the dais.

After the shooting, Thornton's kin found a brief, unsigned note he left on his bed: "The truth will win in the end." It is inconceivable that even Thornton would have considered the carnage a victory. If anything, his actions left chaos, including a deepened divide between white Kirkwood and black Meacham Park. Black residents, while condemning the murders, tried to address what they saw as the underlying reasons for Thornton's actions. White residents could not believe that anyone, white or black, would attempt to rationalize such an irrational act.

Thornton's wife, Maureen, apologized. But she went on to say, "I stand in the aftermath of events that have been going on for more than eight years with the City of Kirkwood. In the middle of a terrible weather change, a tornado or a hurricane, there has to be a force that causes the funnel to move. When you are dealing with forces of good and evil, something causes the funnel to move."

Thornton's mother, Annie Bell Thornton, said, "No one should kill." Then she added, "But people shouldn't drive people to kill."

Kirkwood was changed by the shootings. Some longtime white residents say the Midwestern civility that once defined the city is gone for good. Some longtime black residents respond that it never existed for them.

After the shootings, a Department of Justice mediator worked with citizens to help plot a plan for a more racially harmonious future. In 2010, after a rancorous eighteen-month process, the Kirkwood City Council approved a nonbinding agreement in which the city committed to improve its efforts at human rights and racial equity for residents of Meacham Park.

The agreement did not go far enough for a black group, Kirkwood Citizens for Equity, who pressed unsuccessfully for a preamble that would have acknowledged Kirkwood's culpability for creating a ghetto in Meacham Park "through neglect, discrimination and annexations over the years." These advocates, including Charles Runnels, Cookie Thornton's Men's Breakfast Club friend, sought a more direct link in the document between past racial problems and Thornton's murders—unthinkable to most in Kirkwood.

For his part, Councilman Ward told me that he does not believe racism was at the root of Thornton's treatment by the city, although he added, "Racism is an issue for every city in this nation, not only Kirkwood, Missouri."

Today, Meacham Park sits bookended between the Kirkwood Commons mall to the west and Sam's Club to the east. I asked Ward, a third-generation Kirkwood resident, whether the neighborhood is improved two decades after annexation.

"Physically, it is a new place," he said. The old Meacham Park was "your worst nightmare" of human and urban decay, he said.

But he acknowledged that gang-driven crime has a fresh grip on the neighborhood, and as a result many residents live in fear, "holed up in their homes." He said, "Everyone has a right to live in safety. That's not what's happening over there now. We still have those struggles. We still have some hurdles to climb."

Ward said the long-term solution for Meacham Park's socioeconomic maladies will come from within families and through productive, empowering engagement between government and citizens who feel forgotten.

"If you feel disenfranchised," Ward told me, "usually that doesn't go away for you."

Kirkwood, Missouri, has Cookie Thornton as enduring proof of that statement.

CHAPTER 11

The Pitiful Barflies and Their Big Score

Their big day began, as usual, with an eye-opener.

Bonnie Heady and her boyfriend, Carl Hall, shooed their boxer dog, Doc, into the station wagon, and at 7:30 A.M. they pulled away from the little Cape Cod-style house where they lived on the eastern edge of St. Joseph, Missouri. Hall drove south on busy Highway 71, and an hour later they were sitting among the morning-shift barflies at one of their regular roadhouses, Lynn's tavern, on the outskirts of Kansas City. They had "a drink or two," Heady later said, which probably means they had three or four. They were the sort of drinkers who marked their alcohol intake by the pint, not by the shot. Before they left, Hall bought a packet of chlorophyll tablets and stuffed a couple of tablets into his tipsy girlfriend's mouth. He didn't want her to smell like a highball. She had important work to do.

Hall guided the Plymouth wagon through downtown Kansas City and down Main Street to Katz Drug Store, on 40th Street. Just as they had planned, Heady got out of the car, hailed a cab, and directed the driver to the lovely, leafy Hyde Park section of Midtown, where they passed stately Tudor and brick homes before turning up the driveway at a campus of distinct blond brick buildings. This was the Notre Dame de Sion Catholic School, at 38th and Locust Streets. Heady arrived at the front door there at 10:55 on that Monday morning, September 28, 1953. Leaving the cab idling outside, the woman went in.

Heady was a stranger there, but she was greeted warmly a nun, Sister Morand. Heady explained with feigned agitation that she had come to fetch Bobby Greenlease, a first-grader at the school. She said the boy's mother, Virginia, had suffered a heart attack that morning and was desperate to see her son. Heady identified herself as an aunt. Mrs. Greenlease was thirty-eight years old, an elegant woman with raven hair, tall and thin as a fashion model. Bonnie Heady was short and thick, with a pasty full-moon face and a scarce chin. She wore frumpy brown clothes and was not particularly well-spoken. She would seem to have absolutely nothing in common with Virginia Greenlease. But the nuns bought her story. It was all so simple, just as her boyfriend had promised.

Sister Morand sent a colleague to get Bobby. Bonnie Heady was led into the chapel, where she and Sister Morand prayed for the well-being of Mrs. Greenlease. Well, the nun prayed. Heady knelt beside her, bowed her head, squinted her eyes, and pretended to talk to God. After a few minutes, little Bobby arrived. He was an affable, sandy-haired six-year-old wearing a Catholic school uniform of brown slacks and a white shirt. His shirt was pinned with a Jerusalem cross, signifying God's reach around the globe.

"He took me by the hand, and we walked out of the front door of the school building and entered the taxicab," Bonnie Heady later said.

Bobby chatted all the way in the cab ride back to Katz Drug Store. He talked about his religious medal, his parrot named Polly, his pet dogs, his family's two Cadillac automobiles. Heady paid the eighty-five-cent fare with a dollar bill. She spied Hall sitting in the

Plymouth at the back of the parking lot, and she and the boy walked to the car.

"Bobby, without any reluctance, got into the station wagon next to Carl, and I got in the front seat to the right of Bobby," Heady said. "As soon as we got into the station wagon, Carl remarked, 'Hello, Bobby. How are you?' And Bobby answered, 'Fine,' or some other similar remark."

The guileless child had no idea what he was in for.

The three continued talking as if they were old friends as Hall drove through the Westport neighborhood, west on Highway 50 across the Missouri-Kansas state line, then five miles farther along until the city faded into farmland in Johnson County, Kansas. Hall pulled the car into a wheatfield obscured from the road by a tall windbreak.

"Here, Bobby Greenlease noticed some large, green hedge balls and made some remark to me about them," Heady explained. "Inasmuch as I knew that was the place where Carl was going to murder the victim, I did not want to be present to witness the actual murdering, so I told Bobby I would get him one of the hedge balls."

She walked away, taking Doc the dog with her. And Carl Hall went to work.

"Bobby was still sitting on the front seat," Hall later said. "I had a piece of rope, which was part of the clothesline I had obtained from Bonnie's home. I then placed this rope around Bobby's neck and endeavored to strangle him. This rope was 12 or 15 inches long and was too short for me to hold in my hand and get a good twist. I realized then that I would be unable to strangle the victim. Bobby was struggling and kicking, so I took my .38-caliber revolver and fired what I believe to be two shots at Bobby's head at close range. I missed him on the first shot, but the second one entered his head, causing him to bleed profusely and subsequently die."

Hall yanked the body out onto the ground to avoid further soiling the car. He wrapped the corpse in a tarp, stowed it on the floorboards of the backseat and waved Heady back to the station wagon. She wiped splattered blood off Hall's face as he drove north, back through Kansas City toward St. Joe. On the way, they again stopped at Lynn's tavern for a drink or two. Heady delivered cocktails to Hall in the parking lot. He was afraid to go inside because his clothes were covered with the child's blood.

With their shakes steadied, they continued back to Heady's house, on an elevated corner lot on South 38th Street in a middling section of St. Joseph. The previous day, Carl Hall had taken eight hours to dig a grave for Bobby beside the back door. (This may have been the only real labor he had done in his thirty-four years. He liked to say that his hands had never had a callous.) After dark, he dropped Bobby's body in the hole, then covered it with a thick layer of lime and three feet of dirt. He masked the grave by planting mums purchased earlier for that purpose. Finished at last, the lovers turned out the porch light. The first step in their get-rich kidnapping scheme was complete. Bobby Greenlease was dead.

Virginia and Robert Cosgrove Greenlease Sr. learned of the abduction forty-five minutes after it happened, at about the time that Carl Hall ended the boy's life, when a nun phoned their mansion on Verona Road in Mission Hills, Kansas, to check on the mother's condition. Filled with dread, Robert Sr. rushed home from work.

Robert Greenlease was everything that Carl Hall was not: ambitious, industrious, and honest. He was born on a Missouri farm in 1882, in the horse-and-buggy days. He moved to Kansas City as an adolescent and became enthralled by the entrepreneurial potential of the horseless carriages that were beginning to show up on the rutted city streets of America. Not yet twenty-one, Greenlease and a partner designed an automobile they dubbed the Kansas City Hummer. That venture failed, and he briefly sold another brand, the Buffalo-based Thomas Flyer, before picking a winner with Detroit's Cadillac, America's premier luxury motor car even then. Greenlease won a franchise from Cadillac, and his name eventually became synonymous with the brand in the Midwest. He owned Cadillac and Oldsmobile dealerships in Kansas City, Tulsa, Oklahoma City, Omaha, and Topeka, and he became a distributor of the Cadillac brand to dealers from the Dakotas to south Texas. His

Greenlease Cadillac showroom at 3200 Main Street became a Kansas City icon. Over time, his automobile empire—and hard work—made him very rich.

Greenlease married young, but he was disappointed when he and his wife failed to conceive a child. They adopted a son, Paul, when Greenlease was thirty-five. The boy had all good things in life, including a boarding-school education at Kemper Military Academy in Boonville, Missouri, known as the West Point of the Midwest. When his marriage failed in middle age, Greenlease embarked on a romance with a registered nurse young enough to be his daughter. He wed the woman, Kansas City native Virginia Pollock, in 1939. He was fifty-eight years old, precisely twice her age. A daughter, Virginia Sue, arrived two years later, and Bobby was born in 1947, when his father was sixty-five. The children grew up amid servants and chauffeurs in the thirty-room, 12,000-square-foot Mission Hills mansion. Virginia Greenlease was a devout Catholic, and she became a fixture at St. Agnes Catholic Church in nearby Roeland Park, Kansas. Virginia Sue was enrolled at the exclusive Sunset Hill Girl's School in the Kansas City Plaza, and Bobby became a pupil at the French-run Notre Dame de Sion in Hyde Park.

When his son went missing, Robert Greenlease was unequivocal about one thing: No price was too high to pay for the boy's safe return.

The kidnapping was a remarkable feat for Bonnie Heady and Carl Hall, who were not the sort of people accustomed to accomplishment, good or bad.

They met in May 1953, just months before the crime was committed, when Hall parked himself on a barstool beside Heady at the Pony Express Saloon in downtown St. Joe's Hotel Robidoux, once the gem of the old rough-and-tumble stockyards town.

Heady, forty-one, had reached a crossroad in life and made a wrong turn.

She was born Bonnie Brown in 1912 on a farm in Burlington Junction, Missouri, in the northwest corner of the state, a ten-minute drive from Iowa. Her mother died when Bonnie was a toddler, and she was raised by an aunt, who described the girl's childhood as happy and carefree. At age twenty-one she married Vernon Heady. The couple moved to St. Joseph, where Vernon worked as a trader at the Livestock Exchange Building, which stood amidst the lowing and bustle of the city's busy stockyards, on the Missouri River south of town. Childless in a seventeen-year marriage, they occupied their spare time by raising show-quality boxer dogs and purebred quarter horses.

Bonnie Heady's life turned in 1950. She had always enjoyed her whiskey, but her drinking had gone from social to obsessive, and Vernon finally had had enough. He filed for divorce, and Bonnie got their South 38th Street home in an acrimonious divorce. She descended quickly into a perilous lifestyle. Within months, she had repurposed a spare bedroom into a sex parlor. Bonnie Heady wasn't good looking, but she was available. Soon, St. Joe cabbies and bartenders were directing lonely men to her back door for $10 tricks. By the time she met Hall a few years later, she was a sexual professional.

Carl Hall, born in Kansas City in 1919, grew up seventy-five miles to the south in Pleasanton, Kansas (pop. 1,000), where his father established a law practice. His parents, John and Zella, gave little Carl their full attention after they lost their only other child, who was severely handicapped, at age five.

"No one could have a finer mother than I had, and the same goes for my father," Hall said. "I had wonderful parents. Their actions were in no way responsible for my going bad."

John Hall fell victim to a fatal brain tumor in 1932. The following year, Carl was sent away to Kemper Military Academy, where his classmates included Paul Greenlease, the adopted son of Robert Greenlease. Hall got a good start at Kemper, known like all military schools for its strict regimen and discipline. During his first two years there, he got good grades, played sports, and was described in evaluations with adjectives like dependable, conscientious, ambitious, and honest.

All that changed in his third year. Instructors began characterizing the teenager as temperamental, duplicitous. "Tries to bluff," said one teacher. "Worthless streak," wrote another.

Hall had discovered alcohol, and he was one of those teenagers who found it simply irresistible. He was invited to leave Kemper and spent his senior year at Pleasanton High School. When he managed to get a diploma in 1937, his mother dreamed that Hall would attend a good college and then law school, like his father and grandfather. But he had none of their initiative. He flunked out of a Baptist college (after getting a girl pregnant) and joined the Marine Corps in 1938. He served two four-year stints during the World War II era, making sergeant before being busted back to corporal for his frequent booze binges. He was discharged in 1946 "under honorable conditions"—a military designation regarded as less savory than the traditional honorable discharge.

He returned home a wealthy young man. His mother died in 1944, while Hall was away, and he inherited a handsome home on West 10th Street in Pleasanton and 1,200 acres of prime farmland nearby. The estate was worth more than $200,000—roughly $2 million in today's money. With shrewd investment, he might have been set for life. But Hall was not the shrewd sort.

After a quick marriage and even quicker divorce, he converted his inheritance to cash, moved to the luxurious Phillips Hotel in Kansas City, and proceeded to spend like a drunken sailor—on booze, women, and gambling. There were all manner of people in Kansas City available to relieve Hall of his inheritance bounty. The city was booming in the late 1940s. Its thriving downtown became a regional hub of banking and commerce for farmers, ranchers, and businessmen, and the teeming stockyards in adjacent West Bottoms grew to become America's second largest, after Chicago. And as in Chicago, organized crime had its own shadow enterprises in the dark corners of the city. Mobsters and molls smiled when Carl Hall walked into a saloon or a card game. In five years, his bank accounts were depleted, his inheritance stake gone.

Hall began contemplating an infusion of easy cash from another source. He tried robbery but failed at that, too. In the summer of 1951, he pulled a series of eight taxicab stickups that netted a total of $33—less than half a sawbuck each. He was arrested and locked up on a five-year sentence that lasted fifteen months. Hall was paroled on April 24, 1953, and a lawyer friend of his father set him up with a cheap apartment and a job selling life insurance in St. Joseph, safely upriver and apart from the more abundant temptations of Kansas City.

Carl Hall sold one insurance policy: to Bonnie Heady. They were a couple by the time they staggered out of St. Joe's Pony Express Saloon on that May day, a month after Hall's parole. They went home to Heady's sex den, and Hall simply never left. They were stuck together like gum on shoe leather.

What did they see in one another? Neither could be described as attractive. They were soft, flabby people. Heady was prematurely middle-aged, and Hall's rapidly receding widow's peak made him seem much older than thirty-four. They did have two things in common: dishonesty and alcohol. He became Bonnie's "Honeybunch." She was his "Baby Doll." The relationship would last about eight months before justice intervened. Heady was later asked to describe their life together. She had a curious take.

"Carl and I," she said, "lived a life of leisure."

In fact, Hall and Heady spent most of their time drinking whiskey—generally, at least a fifth per day for each of them. And in the rare moments when they weren't drunk, they were planning and executing one of the most inscrutable acts in the annals of American crime: the murder of Bobby Greenlease.

Child snatchings for profit have happened throughout recorded human history, dating back more than two thousand years. The American prototype was the abduction of Charley Ross, age four, in Philadelphia on July 1, 1874. The son of a wealthy merchant, Charley was snatched off the street and spirited away in a carriage. The boy's father received twenty-three ransom notes demanding $20,000. He wanted to pay, but the local authorities urged Ross to avoid establishing a precedent by giving in to the financial demand. They believed that would lead to many copycat kidnappings. Ross didn't pay, the ransom notes stopped, and the child was never seen again. Thereafter, wealthy fathers became much more inclined to pay, and to pay quickly.

A generation later, a teenager named Eddie Cudahy, heir to a meat-packing fortune, was kidnapped three hours north of Kansas City in Omaha, Nebraska. He was released after his father paid $25,000. Other notable cases included the 1909 snatching of Billy Whitla, son of a Pennsylvania steel baron, who was released when his father paid a $10,000 ransom; the horrible "thrill-kill" kidnapping of Bobby Franks, fourteen, by college students Richard Loeb and Nathan Leopold in Chicago in 1924; and the 1927 snatching and murder of Marian Parker, twelve, daughter of a Los Angeles banker, which led to the first execution of a kidnapper in modern America.

Kidnapping-for-profit was a scourge in the United States during the 1930s. There were three headline cases in Kansas City alone during this decade, involving the children of a drug company executive, the head of a clothing firm, and the city manager. In each instance, a ransom was paid and the captive released unharmed. Of course, the totemic American kidnapping was the 1932 abduction and murder of Charles Lindbergh's son in New Jersey, which led to the federal Kidnapping Act that gave jurisdiction to the FBI (and its press-loving boss, J. Edgar Hoover).

The Philadelphia authorities who counseled Charley Ross's father against paying a ransom were right, in a sense. Kidnapping is a copycat crime, with ebbs and flows based upon publicity. A handful of new cases often follow within months of a marquee example that gains broad press attention. Reports of kidnappings rose in the U.S. in the 1930s, ebbed in the 1940s, and then rose again in the 1950s.

Lacking the motivation for legitimate employment, Carl Hall saw kidnapping as the next best thing to a second inheritance. As he later explained, "I have had it in mind for at least two years. I believed that kidnapping was the one crime I could commit once and obtain a large sum of money."

A few weeks after they met, Hall let Bonnie Heady in on his plans for the big score. She signed on. Trying to come up with a likely victim, Hall reckoned back to his days at Kemper Military Academy and his classmate Paul Greenlease. He knew from reading the Kansas City society pages that Robert Greenlease had remarried and fathered two children, and he began plotting to snatch the daughter, Virginia Sue. He phoned the family's Mission Hills home in August 1953 and elicited from a maid that the Greenleases were vacationing in Europe and would return in time for the start of school in September. When the family got back, Hall cased the Cadillac dealership, the Greenlease home, and the children's schools to discern their daily patterns of coming and going. He followed Mrs. Greenlease's powder-blue Caddy nearly every day for two weeks.

While tailing Virginia Greenlease and her daughter on an errand in mid-September, Hall nearly tried a spontaneous snatch of Virginia Sue when she was left alone in the car outside a store. But he had second thoughts at the last moment, judging the twelve-year-old girl to be too mature and too strong. He began to focus instead on her younger brother, Bobby.

In days leading up to September 28, Hall made extensive preparations. He bought a shovel, a tarp, lime for the grave, a pawn-shop revolver and ammunition, and stamped envelopes and paper for the ransom notes. He also spent time considering the amount of ransom that he would seek. He believed that Robert Greenlease Sr. would be willing to pay $1 million for the boy, but he decided to ask for $600,000.

As he explained, "I arrived at this figure because I had previously read in some magazine or other periodical an article giving the weight and size of a package containing a million dollars in $10 and $20 bills. I recalled that a million dollars would be too bulky to handle but that $600,000 in $10 and $20 bills would weigh approximately 80 to 85 pounds. I thought if this amount were placed in a duffel bag, it would not be too awkward or unwieldy for me to handle in comparative safety."

With that decision made and his preparations in their final stages, Hall had one overriding concern: the fitness of Bonnie Heady.

FBI Agent Donald Hostetter later wrote, "He further advised that due to her alcoholic mind, she would be in a haze for days, and . . . that she would drink at least a pint of whiskey before breakfast. He stated that his only fear at the particular time was that Mrs. Bonnie Heady was not getting his instructions through her drunken mind and would foul up things at the crucial time when it came time to obtain the victim."

But Heady performed her role flawlessly, and the nuns naïvely did their part by sending Bobby Greenlease away with her. A ransom note written by hand on heavy linen paper arrived by mail at the Greenlease home on the day after Bobby was removed from school:

Your boy has been kidnapped get $600,000 in $20's—$10's—Fed. Res. notes from all twelve districts we realize it takes a few days to get that amount. Boy will be in good hands—when you have money ready put ad in K.C. Star. M—will meet you in Chicago next Sunday—signed Mr. G.

Do not call police or try to use chemicals on bills or take numbers. Do not try to use any radio to catch us or boy dies. If you try to trip us your wife and your child and yourself will be killed you will be watched all of the time. You will be told later how to contact us with money. When you get this note let us know by driving up and down main St. between 39 and 29 for twenty minutes with white rag on car aeriel [*sic*].

If do exactly as we say and try no tricks, your boy will be back safe within 24 hrs after we check money.

Deliver money in army duefel [*sic*] bag. Be ready to deliver at once on contact.

M.

$400,000 in 20's

$200,000 in 10's

Robert Greenlease began assembling the cash with the help of his friend Arthur Eisenhower, a Kansas City banker and brother of President Dwight Eisenhower. The FBI made a record of the serial numbers by systematically photographing all 40,000 bills—20,000 each of $20s and $10s. Greenlease placed the ad in the *Star* with the coded message that the money was ready. In the meantime, he received a second, similar ransom letter containing his son's Jerusalem medal. Confused, Greenlease decided to send the kidnapper a message through the press, which had assembled outside his house, to assure them that he was willing to pay. "We think they are trying to make contact," Greenlease said of the kidnappers. "All I want is my boy back."

Although he was ready to pay the ransom, Greenlease had a difficult time figuring out where and when that might happen. Using a phone booth in Kansas City, Hall telephoned the Greenlease home at 9 P.M. Wednesday, fifty-eight hours after the boy was abducted, and asked the family to prepare for a ransom drop Thursday night. It was the beginning of a long series of befuddling messages from the kidnapper. Thursday night came and went without further contact. The next call came at 6:30 P.M. Friday, but the skittish Hall hung up abruptly, after saying that Bobby was "fine but homesick."

Seven hours later, at 1:30 A.M. Saturday, Hall called again to direct Greenlease to a series of scavenger-hunt notes left beneath mailboxes in midtown Kansas City. The final note instructed a money drop outside a church, but the Greenlease contingent did not have the cash with them because they thought they were merely getting instructions and not making the drop. They returned to Mission Hills. Hall called again at 4 A.M. to ask what had gone wrong, and Greenlease explained he was confused by the instructions. Hall vowed to do better.

He phoned again at 12:14 A.M. Sunday. It was a cruel conversation as the frantic Virginia Greenlease begged for confirmation of her son's well-being.

Hall said, "We have the boy. He is alive. Believe me, he's been driving us nuts. . . We have treated him very well. . . We'll carry out our bargain if you carry yours out. I assure you your boy is safe. He is a hellcat. Lady, we have earned this money."

Seventy minutes later, he phoned with new convoluted ransom-drop instructions that directed the family to 13th and Summit Streets, then to a side road in the country off Highway 169. Family friends making the drop did their best to follow the directions, leaving the $600,000 beside the road at what they believed was the designated location.

But Hall couldn't find the money. He phoned again at 4:32 A.M., and the Greenlease friends hurried out into the night to retrieve the cash—which lay undisturbed. Hall, sounding drunk, called repeatedly that day. Robert Greenlease's emissary, his business associate and friend William Ledterman, finally snapped at him.

"Let's get this thing over!" Ledterman said. "This idea of climbing the tree and looking in a bird's nest for a note, then climbing on your belly somewhere looking for something under a rock with a red, white and blue ribbon around it—that's getting tiresome. You know, you and I don't have to play ball that way. We can deal man to man."

Hall hiccupped a reply: "There will be no mix-up tonight. It will go perfectly."

At 12:35 A.M. on Monday, October 5, a week after the kidnapping, Ledterman dropped the money again east of Kansas City beside a bridge on a county road off busy Highway 40. A few minutes later, Hall and Heady picked up the $600,000. As they headed east across Missouri, Hall paused at a pay phone to call the Greenleases with one last heartless lie.

He told Ledterman, "You can tell his mother that she will see him as we promised within twenty-four hours." He said he would send a telegram with details of the release to Western Union in Pittsburg, Kansas.

Ledterman asked, "The boy is alive and well?"

Hall said, "And as full of piss as any kid I've ever seen."

"I can quote you on that, can I?" said Ledterman.

Hall replied, "Yes, you can quote me."

Ledterman sped the 100 miles south to Pittsburg, where he waited in vain.

Against all odds, two addled barflies had managed to pull off a kidnapping and murder, and then extract a record ransom. What they did afterward makes their evil accomplishment even more unlikely. In a sedan they had rented in St. Joseph, Heady and Hall drove across Missouri on Highway 40 to St. Louis. This was the extent of their getaway plan—to drive across the state. They had no luggage, not even a toothbrush and a change of clothes. They had nothing but $600,000 and an unquenchable thirst.

They arrived in St. Louis just in time for a sunrise eye-opener at the first beer joint they found, the Sportsman's Bar on South Jefferson Street. They moved on to Slay's tavern on North Broadway. While Heady guzzled whiskey, Hall went to a store nearby and bought a footlocker and suitcase. He transferred the cash from the duffel, and then visited the Hi-Nabor Bar on Wyoming Street. It was their third bar in St. Louis, and it was not yet 10 A.M.

At midday, Hall deposited his passed-out girlfriend at a cheap apartment on Arsenal Street. He left her $2,000 and a note that read, "Had to move bags in a hurry as report came in on radio—Girl next door looked funny—Couldn't wake you—Stay here and I'll call when I can."

He split with the rest of the loot and headed back to the saloons. That afternoon, Hall ended up in a taxi driven by a kindred spirit named Johnny Hager, who doubled as a one-girl pimp. Hall gave Hager $100 to find him a hooker. Hager later explained, "I said to myself, 'What a fare I've got here!' I decided I was going to stick with this guy."

Hager delivered his golden fare and a big blond named Sandy O'Day to Room 49A at the Coral Court, a no-tell motel on Route 66. Hall spread his money around, with lavish tips for Hager, and $200 plus dinner for O'Day. That was another bad investment. By the time they got to bed, O'Day later revealed, Hall was too drunk to perform.

Hager reported for duty to Hall at the Coral Court early the next morning, then spent the day ferrying him around to bars in St. Louis. Thanks to Hager, every mug in St. Louis knew there was an easy mark in town. Hager had called his boss at Ace Cab Company, a mob hanger-on named Joe Costello, to say that his fare was throwing around cash like it was confetti. Costello tipped a corrupt cop, Lt. Lou Shoulders. At 7:30 that night, forty-one hours after Hall got rich quick, Costello, Lieutenant Shoulders, and a cop named Elmer Dolan barged into Hall's room and said, "The gig is up." They arrested Hall, dropped him off for booking, and then vanished for an hour. When they returned to the district police station, they were carrying the footlocker and suitcase, which they entered into evidence. The bags contained just $288,000 in cash. More than half the ransom money was suddenly missing.

Shoulders hadn't immediately made the connection between Hall and the Greenlease case, but he was treated like a hero in the St. Louis press.

"I just thought he was some crook with money to spend, probably from a holdup," Shoulders said. He explained that he made the arrest after he was tipped off by a confidential informant about "a man spending money around the Congress Hotel who doesn't look the type."

Carl Hall fingered his girlfriend, and cops arrested Heady in her rented room. She had been drunk for the entire duration of her affluence.

Heady was the first to talk. She admitted everything in an interview with FBI Agent J. E. Thornton. She said she knew what she did was wrong, but blamed booze and a blind love for Hall. She explained, "I thought if I called the police they'd come and take him [Hall] away, and I love him very much and want to keep him. We had been very happy together."

Confronted with Heady's admissions, Hall said, "It's true."

Each of the partners gave long, detailed confessions (quoted in this account)—thirty-six pages from Carl Hall, twenty-five from Heady.

Every cop who spoke to Hall had one question: Why did he have to kill the boy? He had no good answer, but here is what he said in his confession: "On Sunday, September 27, 1953 [the day before the kidnapping], I had convinced Bonnie that it would be necessary to kill Bobby Greenlease due to the fact [that] if he were released alive, he might be able to identify both of us as well as Bonnie's automobile used in the abduction and her home in St. Joseph." In other words, murder made the job safer and simpler.

After the arrests, the news that Bobby was dead was delivered to the Greenlease home, and a grim clutch of law enforcers shoveled aside the mums on South 38th Street in St. Joseph the next morning, October 7. After an autopsy, the boy got a proper Catholic burial.

Heady and Hall were charged under the federal Lindbergh Act because they kidnapped Greenlease in Missouri, and then crossed a state line to kill him in Kansas. The venue of the trial was a moot point. The murder was so vile and the confessions so thorough that they would have faced the ultimate comeuppance in any court, state or federal. They pleaded guilty in a gambit to avoid execution, and a jury was convened November 16, just seven weeks after the crime, to decide their fate. The prosecutor read Bonnie Heady's confession to the jury, and an FBI agent read Hall's—each while Robert Greenlease Sr. sat glowering just steps away from the killers. It was the briefest of deliberations when it came to Hall. Jurors condemned him to die after just eight minutes of discussion. The decision on Heady took about an hour because a single juror was at first inclined to spare her. In the end, she was condemned, as well.

Greenlease Sr. said of the verdict, "It's too good for them, but it is the best the law provides."

The killers were rushed to Jefferson City prison to await their fate. They would not wait long. In the meantime, Heady wrote to the Greenlease family, hoping they would have mercy and intercede on her behalf:

I doubt if this letter will do much good, but there isn't anything we could do or say that would atone for our mistake. . . I would give anything if I could go back to that Sunday in September and erase everything that has happened since. It all seems like a nightmare to me. . . I don't say I don't enjoy money, as everybody does, but that was not my motive. I could have been very, very happy with Carl living in my house as I had been, but he was used to more money. My case was loving not wisely, but too well. I wanted so much for him to be happy. . . I think anyone will find if you drink from one to two fifths of whiskey a day for a year and half that your brain doesn't function properly. Since I have been in jail is the first time I've been able to reason clearly for some time."

She was correct: The letter didn't do much good. After midnight on December 18, 1953, a month after sentencing and just eighty-one days after the murder, prison officials led Hall and Heady to the gas chamber. They were allowed ten minutes alone to say goodbye, and then they were blindfolded and strapped into adjacent chairs. Just before the fatal gas flowed, Bonnie Heady said, "Are you doing all right, honey?" Carl Hall replied, "Yes, mama." These were their last words.

A few weeks after Lieutenant Shoulders arrested Hall and delivered only half the ransom money, he left his wife, quit the police force, and went on vacation to Hawaii with a new girlfriend. He said, "I'm tired of being a cop." Asked what might have become of the missing $300,000, he grumbled, "No comment."

After the executions, Shoulders and Officer Dolan were convicted of perjury in connection with the missing loot. Dolan got two years in prison, Shoulders three. Joe Costello, the cab company owner, was not indicted after invoking the Fifth Amendment against self-implication. Cabbie Johnny Hager cooperated with prosecutors and was not charged.

The money recovered was returned to Robert Greenlease. But the missing cash was a niggling source of anger for FBI Director J. Edgar Hoover, who kept an agent assigned exclusively to that investigation for fifteen years. Only 115 of the 16,971 missing bills ever showed up in circulation. In 1962, when both Shoulders and Costello died, Elmer Dolan finally gave in to Hoover's badgering and confessed. He said Shoulders gave half the money to Costello, who laundered it through the St. Louis mob. Dolan said he got just $1,500 for his role, and Shoulders as much as $50,000. At Hoover's urging, President Lyndon Johnson pardoned Elmer Dolan.

After the Greenlease murder, Hoover asked schools to tighten procedures for removal of students by non-parents. The stringent protocols in place today at virtually every school in America, which likely would have saved Bobby Greenlease, are a part of the child's legacy. Another legacy is Rockhurst College in Kansas City, down the road from his final resting place, the Abbey Mausoleum at Forest Hills Cemetery.

Virginia and Robert Greenlease drew comfort from the Rev. Joseph Freeman, a Jesuit priest at Rockhurst, and they paid the school back for the priest's kindness, funding a permanent professorship in Freeman's honor and donating generously in many other ways. They funded a library and art gallery and donated land for a new affiliate high school, naming the property the Greenlease Memorial Campus.

Robert Greenlease Sr. died at age eighty-seven on September 17, 1969, sixteen years after the murder of his son. Virginia died at ninety-one on September 24, 2001, five days short of the forty-eighth anniversary of the crime. She left $1 million each to Rockhurst College and Rockhurst High School in the names of her husband and her son.

Bibliography

Brown, Cecil. *Stagolee Shot Billy*. Cambridge, MA: Harvard University Press, 2004.

Cummins, Jeanine. *A Rip in Heaven: A Memoir of Murder And Its Aftermath*. New York: NAL Trade, 2004.

Deakin, James. *A Grave for Bobby*. New York: William Morrow/Berkeley, 1990.

Fass, Paula. *Kidnapped: Child Abduction in America*. Cambridge, MA: Harvard University Press, 1999.

Granger, Shawn, Brent Giles, and Stefano Cardoselli. *Family Bones Volume 2*. Hollywood, CA: King Tractor Press, 2010.

Kuban, Bob, and Nancy K. Wagner. *My Side of the Bandstand*. St. Louis: Epic, 2006.

Lancaster, Bob, and B. C. Hall. *Judgment Day*. New York: Seaview/Putnam, 1983.

MacLean, Harry N. *In Broad Daylight: A Murder in Skidmore, Missouri*. New York: Dell, 1988.

Miller, Tom. *The Copeland Killers: The Bizarre True Account of Ray and Faye Copeland, the Oldest Couple Ever Sentenced to Death in America*. St. Louis: Pinnacle, 1993.

Priesmeyer, Scottie. *The Cheaters: The Walter Scott Murder*. Oxford, UK: Tula Publishing, 1997.

Bibliography